My digital life

USERNAME/PASSWORD ORGANIZER

Let Family Know®

This organizer belongs to:

A helpful resource

Experts advise to **store PINs and passwords to accounts where you access sensitive information – like financial and retail** – in a separate, secure place away from whatever primary username/password organizer you use. ***The My digital life PRIVATE ACCESS KEEPER*** is designed to help you do just that.

More than PINs and Passwords
It also includes a section for listing combinations, passcodes, location of keys, and other types of information you need to keep private.

Let Family Know® LLC is dedicated to helping people organize the information that matters. The *My Digital Life USERNAME/PASSWORD ORGANIZER* gives you a place to manage logins to online accounts, email, social media, favorite websites, online affiliate income, cloud storage, music collections, video and photo storage and more. This will make it convenient for you, but will also be extremely important for your loved ones someday.

ISBN# 978-1-7334208-4-6

My digital life

USERNAME/PASSWORD ORGANIZER

The My digital life ORGANIZER from Let Family Know® helps you manage logins to online accounts, email, social media, favorite websites, online affiliate income, cloud storage, music collections, video and photo storage and more.

Rule #1: Keep your information safe

While assembling information about your online accounts and passwords is convenient for your day-to-day use – and accessibility will be extremely important for your loved ones someday – please take extra precautions to protect this information.

We live in an era of superhackers, the dark web and data security breaches. Ripping off innocent people is big business and unscrupulous hackers go to great lengths to get information about bank accounts, charge cards, investments, insurance and other personal information. *In the back of this book you'll find a 16-page section packed with tips to help you do just that.*

For websites and online accounts linked to sensitive information – like financial or medical websites– experts recommend you **NEVER** keep your Personal Identification Number (PIN) for an account in the same place where you have the account number stored. And, **NEVER** record a username and password for these types of accounts together.

EXAMPLE: You would list a bank name and information including the account number and user name in this ORGANIZER, BUT, you would list the PIN and password, or password hint, in a separate notebook and put it in a secure place AWAY FROM this main passwords organizer. That is ONE example.

Let Family Know created a ***My Digital Life PRIVATE ACCESS KEEPER*** to complement this book (mentioned on the previous page) – however, an ordinary small notebook can also be used.

This book is arranged in sections

■ Websites and Digital Assets

List the websites you log into most

■ Online Accounts I Pay Into or Collect Money From

This will be especially helpful for family or executors to stop recurring fees quickly – and to know if you have funds coming from online sources.

■ Email Accounts

How many email accounts do you have? How many times do you need to change your password? This makes it easier to keep track.

■ Protecting personal and financial information in the Internet age

Common and not-so-common tips for protecting personal and financial information in the Internet age.

TIPS

Advisors warn NOT to go totally paperless

If you are comfortable creating and storing information in digital formats or online password services, it may be tempting to go completely paperless. But some advisors say it could cost your heirs a lot of time, money and frustration, trying to locate and access your digital accounts when settling your estate. Heirs, or a digital executor if you've assigned one, will need usernames and passwords for doing things like stopping emails, online payments, electronic bank statements; closing social media accounts; managing affiliate income accounts, and more. It's a big job, and this Password organizer can make it a lot less difficult.

Assign a digital executor for your digital assets

Some states have laws governing the handling of digital assets after someone dies. Regardless if yours does or not, consider appointing a digital executor to be in charge of handling your digital assets. They would delete, destroy, download, convert or share files; close your blog or social media profiles, etc., per your instructions.

With huge volumes of information, photos, videos, music collections and more being stored digitally in the cloud, on CD/DVDs or dedicated servers, etc., digital assets can be a lot to manage. A digital executor can help make sure only the people you designate will have information on how to access them.

If you like the flexibility of adding, removing or rearranging pages, here's something you can do.

You can carefully take the pages out of this paperback book and put them into a ring binder. *If you're going to do this, it may be best to do it before writing begins.* An online search for "how to remove pages from a paperback book" will yield several results, including videos.

Heat gun/hair dryer approach

This will warm and loosen the glue holding the paperback book together.

1. Turn your hair dryer on using the higher heat setting. Carefully blow the hot air up and down along the book's spine. The dryer should not be touching the spine. It will take around 3 to 6 minutes to soften the glue so pages will remove easily.
2. When the glue is soft, gently pull the cover away from the spine. The entire cover should easily come off in one piece.
3. You may find it easier to remove the pages in sections. Try to keep them in order. It may be necessary to slightly reheat the glue on the spine of the pages so you can pull off any glue chunks, leaving a clean, smooth edge.
4. Once the pages and glue are removed, you're ready to punch the holes and place the pages in a ring binder. You can put the book covers in as well. Paper punches and planner-size ring binders can be purchased online or in an office supply store.

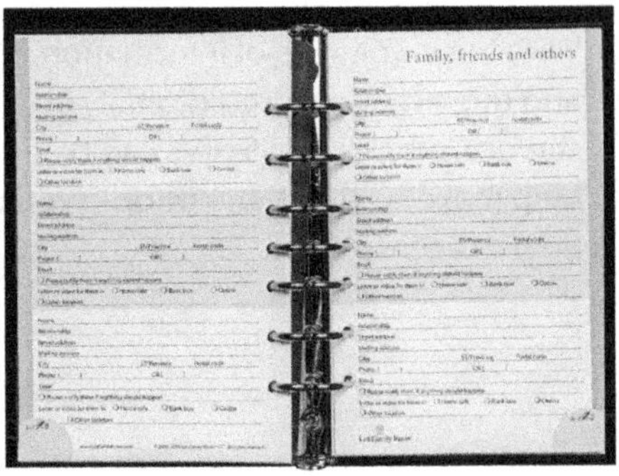

X-acto knife/box knife approach

Lay the book flat open and carefully cut the pages out

So the process goes smoothly, it may be helpful to watch a how-to video before you begin. Once pages are removed, use a paper punch to make holes that match the rings configuration of your binder.

Easiest option

A local print shop or office products store can remove the pages and drill the holes for you, for a small fee.

Websites and Digital Assets

My digital life

General

WEBSITE OR DIGITAL ASSET

❑ website ❑ photo/video/music storage ❑ social media ❑ other

Name of site/asset ______

Website address ______

______

Username/Login ______

______

PIN or Code ______

❑ Password/hint ______

______

Password/hint change ______

______

______

❑ ✔ if password/PIN are recorded in a separate location

WEBSITE OR DIGITAL ASSET

❑ website ❑ photo/video/music storage ❑ social media ❑ other

Name of site/asset ______

Website address ______

______

Username/Login ______

______

PIN or Code ______

❑ Password/hint ______

______

Password/hint change ______

______

______

❑ ✔ if password/PIN are recorded in a separate location

WEBSITE OR DIGITAL ASSET

❑ website ❑ photo/video/music storage ❑ social media ❑ other

Name of site/asset ____________________

Website address ____________________

____

Username/Login ____________________

____

PIN or Code ____________________

❑ Password/hint ____________________

____

Password/hint change ____________________

____

____

❑ ✔ if password/PIN are recorded in a separate location

WEBSITE OR DIGITAL ASSET

❑ website ❑ photo/video/music storage ❑ social media ❑ other

Name of site/asset ____________________

Website address ____________________

____

Username/Login ____________________

____

PIN or Code ____________________

❑ Password/hint ____________________

____

Password/hint change ____________________

____

____

❑ ✔ if password/PIN are recorded in a separate location

My digital life

General

WEBSITE OR DIGITAL ASSET

❑ website ❑ photo/video/music storage ❑ social media ❑ other

Name of site/asset ______________________

Website address ______________________

____

Username/Login ______________________

____

PIN or Code ______________________

❑ Password/hint ______________________

____

Password/hint change ______________________

____

____

❑ ✔ if password/PIN are recorded in a separate location

WEBSITE OR DIGITAL ASSET

❑ website ❑ photo/video/music storage ❑ social media ❑ other

Name of site/asset ______________________

Website address ______________________

____

Username/Login ______________________

____

PIN or Code ______________________

❑ Password/hint ______________________

____

Password/hint change ______________________

____

____

❑ ✔ if password/PIN are recorded in a separate location

WEBSITE OR DIGITAL ASSET

❑ website ❑ photo/video/music storage ❑ social media ❑ other

Name of site/asset ______________________________

Website address ______________________________

Username/Login ______________________________

PIN or Code ______________________________

❑ Password/hint ______________________________

Password/hint change ______________________________

❑ ✔ if password/PIN are recorded in a separate location

WEBSITE OR DIGITAL ASSET

❑ website ❑ photo/video/music storage ❑ social media ❑ other

Name of site/asset ______________________________

Website address ______________________________

Username/Login ______________________________

PIN or Code ______________________________

❑ Password/hint ______________________________

Password/hint change ______________________________

❑ ✔ if password/PIN are recorded in a separate location

My digital life

General

WEBSITE OR DIGITAL ASSET

❑ website ❑ photo/video/music storage ❑ social media ❑ other

Name of site/asset ______

Website address ______

______

Username/Login ______

______

PIN or Code ______

❑ Password/hint ______

______

Password/hint change ______

______

______

❑ ✔ if password/PIN are recorded in a separate location

WEBSITE OR DIGITAL ASSET

❑ website ❑ photo/video/music storage ❑ social media ❑ other

Name of site/asset ______

Website address ______

______

Username/Login ______

______

PIN or Code ______

❑ Password/hint ______

______

Password/hint change ______

______

______

❑ ✔ if password/PIN are recorded in a separate location

WEBSITE OR DIGITAL ASSET

❑ website ❑ photo/video/music storage ❑ social media ❑ other

Name of site/asset ______________________________

Website address ______________________________

____

Username/Login ______________________________

____

PIN or Code ______________________________

❑ Password/hint ______________________________

____

Password/hint change ______________________________

____

____

❑ ✔ if password/PIN are recorded in a separate location

WEBSITE OR DIGITAL ASSET

❑ website ❑ photo/video/music storage ❑ social media ❑ other

Name of site/asset ______________________________

Website address ______________________________

____

Username/Login ______________________________

____

PIN or Code ______________________________

❑ Password/hint ______________________________

____

Password/hint change ______________________________

____

____

❑ ✔ if password/PIN are recorded in a separate location

My digital life

General

WEBSITE OR DIGITAL ASSET

❑ website ❑ photo/video/music storage ❑ social media ❑ other

Name of site/asset ______________________

Website address ______________________

____

Username/Login ______________________

____

PIN or Code ______________________

❑ Password/hint ______________________

____

Password/hint change ______________________

____

____

❑ ✔ if password/PIN are recorded in a separate location

WEBSITE OR DIGITAL ASSET

❑ website ❑ photo/video/music storage ❑ social media ❑ other

Name of site/asset ______________________

Website address ______________________

____

Username/Login ______________________

____

PIN or Code ______________________

❑ Password/hint ______________________

____

Password/hint change ______________________

____

____

❑ ✔ if password/PIN are recorded in a separate location

WEBSITE OR DIGITAL ASSET

❑ website ❑ photo/video/music storage ❑ social media ❑ other

Name of site/asset ______________________

Website address ______________________

____

Username/Login ______________________

____

PIN or Code ______________________

❑ Password/hint ______________________

____

Password/hint change ______________________

____

____

❑ ✔ if password/PIN are recorded in a separate location

WEBSITE OR DIGITAL ASSET

❑ website ❑ photo/video/music storage ❑ social media ❑ other

Name of site/asset ______________________

Website address ______________________

____

Username/Login ______________________

____

PIN or Code ______________________

❑ Password/hint ______________________

____

Password/hint change ______________________

____

____

❑ ✔ if password/PIN are recorded in a separate location

My digital life

General

WEBSITE OR DIGITAL ASSET

❑ website ❑ photo/video/music storage ❑ social media ❑ other

Name of site/asset ______

Website address ______

______

Username/Login ______

______

PIN or Code ______

❑ Password/hint ______

______

Password/hint change ______

______

______

❑ ✔ if password/PIN are recorded in a separate location

WEBSITE OR DIGITAL ASSET

❑ website ❑ photo/video/music storage ❑ social media ❑ other

Name of site/asset ______

Website address ______

______

Username/Login ______

______

PIN or Code ______

❑ Password/hint ______

______

Password/hint change ______

______

______

❑ ✔ if password/PIN are recorded in a separate location

WEBSITE OR DIGITAL ASSET

❑ website ❑ photo/video/music storage ❑ social media ❑ other

Name of site/asset ______________________________

Website address ______________________________

____

Username/Login ______________________________

____

PIN or Code ______________________________

❑ Password/hint ______________________________

____

Password/hint change ______________________________

____

____

❑ ✔ if password/PIN are recorded in a separate location

WEBSITE OR DIGITAL ASSET

❑ website ❑ photo/video/music storage ❑ social media ❑ other

Name of site/asset ______________________________

Website address ______________________________

____

Username/Login ______________________________

____

PIN or Code ______________________________

❑ Password/hint ______________________________

____

Password/hint change ______________________________

____

____

❑ ✔ if password/PIN are recorded in a separate location

My digital life

General

WEBSITE OR DIGITAL ASSET

❑ website ❑ photo/video/music storage ❑ social media ❑ other

Name of site/asset ______________________

Website address ______________________

____

Username/Login ______________________

____

PIN or Code ______________________

❑ Password/hint ______________________

____

Password/hint change ______________________

____

____

❑ ✔ if password/PIN are recorded in a separate location

WEBSITE OR DIGITAL ASSET

❑ website ❑ photo/video/music storage ❑ social media ❑ other

Name of site/asset ______________________

Website address ______________________

____

Username/Login ______________________

____

PIN or Code ______________________

❑ Password/hint ______________________

____

Password/hint change ______________________

____

____

❑ ✔ if password/PIN are recorded in a separate location

WEBSITE OR DIGITAL ASSET

❑ website ❑ photo/video/music storage ❑ social media ❑ other

Name of site/asset ______________________________

Website address ______________________________

____

Username/Login ______________________________

____

PIN or Code ______________________________

❑ Password/hint ______________________________

____

Password/hint change ______________________________

____

____

❑ ✔ if password/PIN are recorded in a separate location

WEBSITE OR DIGITAL ASSET

❑ website ❑ photo/video/music storage ❑ social media ❑ other

Name of site/asset ______________________________

Website address ______________________________

____

Username/Login ______________________________

____

PIN or Code ______________________________

❑ Password/hint ______________________________

____

Password/hint change ______________________________

____

____

❑ ✔ if password/PIN are recorded in a separate location

My digital life

General

WEBSITE OR DIGITAL ASSET

❑ website ❑ photo/video/music storage ❑ social media ❑ other

Name of site/asset ______________________

Website address ______________________

____

Username/Login ______________________

____

PIN or Code ______________________

❑ Password/hint ______________________

____

Password/hint change ______________________

____

____

❑ ✔ if password/PIN are recorded in a separate location

WEBSITE OR DIGITAL ASSET

❑ website ❑ photo/video/music storage ❑ social media ❑ other

Name of site/asset ______________________

Website address ______________________

____

Username/Login ______________________

____

PIN or Code ______________________

❑ Password/hint ______________________

____

Password/hint change ______________________

____

____

❑ ✔ if password/PIN are recorded in a separate location

WEBSITE OR DIGITAL ASSET

❑ website ❑ photo/video/music storage ❑ social media ❑ other

Name of site/asset ______________________________

Website address ______________________________

____

Username/Login ______________________________

____

PIN or Code ______________________________

❑ Password/hint ______________________________

____

Password/hint change ______________________________

____

____

❑ ✔ if password/PIN are recorded in a separate location

WEBSITE OR DIGITAL ASSET

❑ website ❑ photo/video/music storage ❑ social media ❑ other

Name of site/asset ______________________________

Website address ______________________________

____

Username/Login ______________________________

____

PIN or Code ______________________________

❑ Password/hint ______________________________

____

Password/hint change ______________________________

____

____

❑ ✔ if password/PIN are recorded in a separate location

My digital life

General

WEBSITE OR DIGITAL ASSET

❑ website ❑ photo/video/music storage ❑ social media ❑ other

Name of site/asset ______

Website address ______

______

Username/Login ______

______

PIN or Code ______

❑ Password/hint ______

______

Password/hint change ______

______

______

❑ ✔ if password/PIN are recorded in a separate location

WEBSITE OR DIGITAL ASSET

❑ website ❑ photo/video/music storage ❑ social media ❑ other

Name of site/asset ______

Website address ______

______

Username/Login ______

______

PIN or Code ______

❑ Password/hint ______

______

Password/hint change ______

______

______

❑ ✔ if password/PIN are recorded in a separate location

WEBSITE OR DIGITAL ASSET

❑ website ❑ photo/video/music storage ❑ social media ❑ other

Name of site/asset ____________________

Website address ____________________

Username/Login ____________________

PIN or Code ____________________

❑ Password/hint ____________________

Password/hint change ____________________

❑ ✔ if password/PIN are recorded in a separate location

WEBSITE OR DIGITAL ASSET

❑ website ❑ photo/video/music storage ❑ social media ❑ other

Name of site/asset ____________________

Website address ____________________

Username/Login ____________________

PIN or Code ____________________

❑ Password/hint ____________________

Password/hint change ____________________

❑ ✔ if password/PIN are recorded in a separate location

WEBSITE OR DIGITAL ASSET

❑ website ❑ photo/video/music storage ❑ social media ❑ other

Name of site/asset ______

Website address ______

______

Username/Login ______

______

PIN or Code ______

❑ Password/hint ______

______

Password/hint change ______

______

______

❑ ✔ if password/PIN are recorded in a separate location

WEBSITE OR DIGITAL ASSET

❑ website ❑ photo/video/music storage ❑ social media ❑ other

Name of site/asset ______

Website address ______

______

Username/Login ______

______

PIN or Code ______

❑ Password/hint ______

______

Password/hint change ______

______

______

❑ ✔ if password/PIN are recorded in a separate location

WEBSITE OR DIGITAL ASSET

❑ website ❑ photo/video/music storage ❑ social media ❑ other

Name of site/asset ____________________

Website address ____________________

____

Username/Login ____________________

____

PIN or Code ____________________

❑ Password/hint ____________________

____

Password/hint change ____________________

____

____

❑ ✔ if password/PIN are recorded in a separate location

WEBSITE OR DIGITAL ASSET

❑ website ❑ photo/video/music storage ❑ social media ❑ other

Name of site/asset ____________________

Website address ____________________

____

Username/Login ____________________

____

PIN or Code ____________________

❑ Password/hint ____________________

____

Password/hint change ____________________

____

____

❑ ✔ if password/PIN are recorded in a separate location

My digital life

General

WEBSITE OR DIGITAL ASSET

❑ website ❑ photo/video/music storage ❑ social media ❑ other

Name of site/asset ______

Website address ______

Username/Login ______

PIN or Code ______

❑ Password/hint ______

Password/hint change ______

❑ ✔ if password/PIN are recorded in a separate location

WEBSITE OR DIGITAL ASSET

❑ website ❑ photo/video/music storage ❑ social media ❑ other

Name of site/asset ______

Website address ______

Username/Login ______

PIN or Code ______

❑ Password/hint ______

Password/hint change ______

❑ ✔ if password/PIN are recorded in a separate location

WEBSITE OR DIGITAL ASSET

❑ website ❑ photo/video/music storage ❑ social media ❑ other

Name of site/asset ______________________________

Website address ______________________________

____

Username/Login ______________________________

____

PIN or Code ______________________________

❑ Password/hint ______________________________

____

Password/hint change ______________________________

____

____

❑ ✔ if password/PIN are recorded in a separate location

WEBSITE OR DIGITAL ASSET

❑ website ❑ photo/video/music storage ❑ social media ❑ other

Name of site/asset ______________________________

Website address ______________________________

____

Username/Login ______________________________

____

PIN or Code ______________________________

❑ Password/hint ______________________________

____

Password/hint change ______________________________

____

____

❑ ✔ if password/PIN are recorded in a separate location

My digital life

General

WEBSITE OR DIGITAL ASSET

❏ website ❏ photo/video/music storage ❏ social media ❏ other

Name of site/asset ______________________

Website address ______________________

____

Username/Login ______________________

____

PIN or Code ______________________

❏ Password/hint ______________________

____

Password/hint change ______________________

____

____

❏ ✔ if password/PIN are recorded in a separate location

WEBSITE OR DIGITAL ASSET

❏ website ❏ photo/video/music storage ❏ social media ❏ other

Name of site/asset ______________________

Website address ______________________

____

Username/Login ______________________

____

PIN or Code ______________________

❏ Password/hint ______________________

____

Password/hint change ______________________

____

____

❏ ✔ if password/PIN are recorded in a separate location

WEBSITE OR DIGITAL ASSET

❑ website ❑ photo/video/music storage ❑ social media ❑ other

Name of site/asset ____________________

Website address ____________________

____

Username/Login ____________________

____

PIN or Code ____________________

❑ Password/hint ____________________

____

Password/hint change ____________________

____

____

❑ ✔ if password/PIN are recorded in a separate location

WEBSITE OR DIGITAL ASSET

❑ website ❑ photo/video/music storage ❑ social media ❑ other

Name of site/asset ____________________

Website address ____________________

____

Username/Login ____________________

____

PIN or Code ____________________

❑ Password/hint ____________________

____

Password/hint change ____________________

____

____

❑ ✔ if password/PIN are recorded in a separate location

My digital life

General

WEBSITE OR DIGITAL ASSET

❑ website ❑ photo/video/music storage ❑ social media ❑ other

Name of site/asset

Website address

Username/Login

PIN or Code

❑ Password/hint

Password/hint change

❑ ✔ if password/PIN are recorded in a separate location

WEBSITE OR DIGITAL ASSET

❑ website ❑ photo/video/music storage ❑ social media ❑ other

Name of site/asset

Website address

Username/Login

PIN or Code

❑ Password/hint

Password/hint change

❑ ✔ if password/PIN are recorded in a separate location

WEBSITE OR DIGITAL ASSET

❏ website ❏ photo/video/music storage ❏ social media ❏ other

Name of site/asset ______________________

Website address ______________________

____

Username/Login ______________________

____

PIN or Code ______________________

❏ Password/hint ______________________

____

Password/hint change ______________________

____

____

❏ ✔ if password/PIN are recorded in a separate location

WEBSITE OR DIGITAL ASSET

❏ website ❏ photo/video/music storage ❏ social media ❏ other

Name of site/asset ______________________

Website address ______________________

____

Username/Login ______________________

____

PIN or Code ______________________

❏ Password/hint ______________________

____

Password/hint change ______________________

____

____

❏ ✔ if password/PIN are recorded in a separate location

My digital life

General

WEBSITE OR DIGITAL ASSET

❑ website ❑ photo/video/music storage ❑ social media ❑ other

Name of site/asset ____________________

Website address ____________________

____

Username/Login ____________________

____

PIN or Code ____________________

❑ Password/hint ____________________

____

Password/hint change ____________________

____

____

❑ ✔ if password/PIN are recorded in a separate location

WEBSITE OR DIGITAL ASSET

❑ website ❑ photo/video/music storage ❑ social media ❑ other

Name of site/asset ____________________

Website address ____________________

____

Username/Login ____________________

____

PIN or Code ____________________

❑ Password/hint ____________________

____

Password/hint change ____________________

____

____

❑ ✔ if password/PIN are recorded in a separate location

WEBSITE OR DIGITAL ASSET

❑ website ❑ photo/video/music storage ❑ social media ❑ other

Name of site/asset ____________________

Website address ____________________

____

Username/Login ____________________

____

PIN or Code ____________________

❑ Password/hint ____________________

____

Password/hint change ____________________

____

____

❑ ✔ if password/PIN are recorded in a separate location

WEBSITE OR DIGITAL ASSET

❑ website ❑ photo/video/music storage ❑ social media ❑ other

Name of site/asset ____________________

Website address ____________________

____

Username/Login ____________________

____

PIN or Code ____________________

❑ Password/hint ____________________

____

Password/hint change ____________________

____

____

❑ ✔ if password/PIN are recorded in a separate location

My digital life

General

WEBSITE OR DIGITAL ASSET

❑ website ❑ photo/video/music storage ❑ social media ❑ other

Name of site/asset ______________________

Website address ______________________

____

Username/Login ______________________

____

PIN or Code ______________________

❑ Password/hint ______________________

____

Password/hint change ______________________

____

____

❑ ✔ if password/PIN are recorded in a separate location

WEBSITE OR DIGITAL ASSET

❑ website ❑ photo/video/music storage ❑ social media ❑ other

Name of site/asset ______________________

Website address ______________________

____

Username/Login ______________________

____

PIN or Code ______________________

❑ Password/hint ______________________

____

Password/hint change ______________________

____

____

❑ ✔ if password/PIN are recorded in a separate location

E

WEBSITE OR DIGITAL ASSET

❑ website ❑ photo/video/music storage ❑ social media ❑ other

Name of site/asset ______________________

Website address ______________________

____

Username/Login ______________________

____

PIN or Code ______________________

❑ Password/hint ______________________

____

Password/hint change ______________________

____

____

❑ ✔ if password/PIN are recorded in a separate location

WEBSITE OR DIGITAL ASSET

❑ website ❑ photo/video/music storage ❑ social media ❑ other

Name of site/asset ______________________

Website address ______________________

____

Username/Login ______________________

____

PIN or Code ______________________

❑ Password/hint ______________________

____

Password/hint change ______________________

____

____

❑ ✔ if password/PIN are recorded in a separate location

My digital life

General

WEBSITE OR DIGITAL ASSET

❑ website ❑ photo/video/music storage ❑ social media ❑ other

Name of site/asset ______________________

Website address ______________________

____

Username/Login ______________________

____

PIN or Code ______________________

❑ Password/hint ______________________

____

Password/hint change ______________________

____

____

❑ ✔ if password/PIN are recorded in a separate location

WEBSITE OR DIGITAL ASSET

❑ website ❑ photo/video/music storage ❑ social media ❑ other

Name of site/asset ______________________

Website address ______________________

____

Username/Login ______________________

____

PIN or Code ______________________

❑ Password/hint ______________________

____

Password/hint change ______________________

____

____

❑ ✔ if password/PIN are recorded in a separate location

WEBSITE OR DIGITAL ASSET

❑ website ❑ photo/video/music storage ❑ social media ❑ other

Name of site/asset ____________________

Website address ____________________

____

Username/Login ____________________

____

PIN or Code ____________________

❑ Password/hint ____________________

____

Password/hint change ____________________

____

____

❑ ✔ if password/PIN are recorded in a separate location

WEBSITE OR DIGITAL ASSET

❑ website ❑ photo/video/music storage ❑ social media ❑ other

Name of site/asset ____________________

Website address ____________________

____

Username/Login ____________________

____

PIN or Code ____________________

❑ Password/hint ____________________

____

Password/hint change ____________________

____

____

❑ ✔ if password/PIN are recorded in a separate location

My digital life

General

WEBSITE OR DIGITAL ASSET

❑ website ❑ photo/video/music storage ❑ social media ❑ other

Name of site/asset ______________________

Website address ______________________

____

Username/Login ______________________

____

PIN or Code ______________________

❑ Password/hint ______________________

____

Password/hint change ______________________

____

____

❑ ✔ if password/PIN are recorded in a separate location

WEBSITE OR DIGITAL ASSET

❑ website ❑ photo/video/music storage ❑ social media ❑ other

Name of site/asset ______________________

Website address ______________________

____

Username/Login ______________________

____

PIN or Code ______________________

❑ Password/hint ______________________

____

Password/hint change ______________________

____

____

❑ ✔ if password/PIN are recorded in a separate location

WEBSITE OR DIGITAL ASSET

❑ website ❑ photo/video/music storage ❑ social media ❑ other

Name of site/asset ______________________

Website address ______________________

____

Username/Login ______________________

____

PIN or Code ______________________

❑ Password/hint ______________________

____

Password/hint change ______________________

____

____

❑ ✔ if password/PIN are recorded in a separate location

WEBSITE OR DIGITAL ASSET

❑ website ❑ photo/video/music storage ❑ social media ❑ other

Name of site/asset ______________________

Website address ______________________

____

Username/Login ______________________

____

PIN or Code ______________________

❑ Password/hint ______________________

____

Password/hint change ______________________

____

____

❑ ✔ if password/PIN are recorded in a separate location

My digital life

General

WEBSITE OR DIGITAL ASSET

❑ website ❑ photo/video/music storage ❑ social media ❑ other

Name of site/asset ______________________

Website address ______________________

____

Username/Login ______________________

____

PIN or Code ______________________

❑ Password/hint ______________________

____

Password/hint change ______________________

____

____

❑ ✔ if password/PIN are recorded in a separate location

WEBSITE OR DIGITAL ASSET

❑ website ❑ photo/video/music storage ❑ social media ❑ other

Name of site/asset ______________________

Website address ______________________

____

Username/Login ______________________

____

PIN or Code ______________________

❑ Password/hint ______________________

____

Password/hint change ______________________

____

____

❑ ✔ if password/PIN are recorded in a separate location

WEBSITE OR DIGITAL ASSET

❑ website ❑ photo/video/music storage ❑ social media ❑ other

Name of site/asset ______________________

Website address ______________________

____

Username/Login ______________________

____

PIN or Code ______________________

❑ Password/hint ______________________

____

Password/hint change ______________________

____

____

❑ ✔ if password/PIN are recorded in a separate location

WEBSITE OR DIGITAL ASSET

❑ website ❑ photo/video/music storage ❑ social media ❑ other

Name of site/asset ______________________

Website address ______________________

____

Username/Login ______________________

____

PIN or Code ______________________

❑ Password/hint ______________________

____

Password/hint change ______________________

____

____

❑ ✔ if password/PIN are recorded in a separate location

My digital life

General

WEBSITE OR DIGITAL ASSET

❏ website ❏ photo/video/music storage ❏ social media ❏ other

Name of site/asset ______________________

Website address ______________________

____

Username/Login ______________________

____

PIN or Code ______________________

❏ Password/hint ______________________

____

Password/hint change ______________________

____

____

❏ ✔ if password/PIN are recorded in a separate location

WEBSITE OR DIGITAL ASSET

❏ website ❏ photo/video/music storage ❏ social media ❏ other

Name of site/asset ______________________

Website address ______________________

____

Username/Login ______________________

____

PIN or Code ______________________

❏ Password/hint ______________________

____

Password/hint change ______________________

____

____

❏ ✔ if password/PIN are recorded in a separate location

WEBSITE OR DIGITAL ASSET

❑ website ❑ photo/video/music storage ❑ social media ❑ other

Name of site/asset ____________________

Website address ____________________

____

Username/Login ____________________

____

PIN or Code ____________________

❑ Password/hint ____________________

____

Password/hint change ____________________

____

____

❑ ✔ if password/PIN are recorded in a separate location

WEBSITE OR DIGITAL ASSET

❑ website ❑ photo/video/music storage ❑ social media ❑ other

Name of site/asset ____________________

Website address ____________________

____

Username/Login ____________________

____

PIN or Code ____________________

❑ Password/hint ____________________

____

Password/hint change ____________________

____

____

❑ ✔ if password/PIN are recorded in a separate location

My digital life

General

WEBSITE OR DIGITAL ASSET

❑ website ❑ photo/video/music storage ❑ social media ❑ other

Name of site/asset

Website address

Username/Login

PIN or Code

❑ Password/hint

Password/hint change

❑ ✔ if password/PIN are recorded in a separate location

WEBSITE OR DIGITAL ASSET

❑ website ❑ photo/video/music storage ❑ social media ❑ other

Name of site/asset

Website address

Username/Login

PIN or Code

❑ Password/hint

Password/hint change

❑ ✔ if password/PIN are recorded in a separate location

WEBSITE OR DIGITAL ASSET

❑ website ❑ photo/video/music storage ❑ social media ❑ other

Name of site/asset ______________________

Website address ______________________

____

Username/Login ______________________

____

PIN or Code ______________________

❑ Password/hint ______________________

____

Password/hint change ______________________

____

____

❑ ✔ if password/PIN are recorded in a separate location

WEBSITE OR DIGITAL ASSET

❑ website ❑ photo/video/music storage ❑ social media ❑ other

Name of site/asset ______________________

Website address ______________________

____

Username/Login ______________________

____

PIN or Code ______________________

❑ Password/hint ______________________

____

Password/hint change ______________________

____

____

❑ ✔ if password/PIN are recorded in a separate location

My digital life

General

WEBSITE OR DIGITAL ASSET

❑ website ❑ photo/video/music storage ❑ social media ❑ other

Name of site/asset __________

Website address __________

____

Username/Login __________

____

PIN or Code __________

❑ Password/hint __________

____

Password/hint change __________

____

____

❑ ✔ if password/PIN are recorded in a separate location

WEBSITE OR DIGITAL ASSET

❑ website ❑ photo/video/music storage ❑ social media ❑ other

Name of site/asset __________

Website address __________

____

Username/Login __________

____

PIN or Code __________

❑ Password/hint __________

____

Password/hint change __________

____

____

❑ ✔ if password/PIN are recorded in a separate location

WEBSITE OR DIGITAL ASSET

❑ website ❑ photo/video/music storage ❑ social media ❑ other

Name of site/asset ______________________________

Website address ______________________________

____

Username/Login ______________________________

____

PIN or Code ______________________________

❑ Password/hint ______________________________

____

Password/hint change ______________________________

____

____

❑ ✔ if password/PIN are recorded in a separate location

WEBSITE OR DIGITAL ASSET

❑ website ❑ photo/video/music storage ❑ social media ❑ other

Name of site/asset ______________________________

Website address ______________________________

____

Username/Login ______________________________

____

PIN or Code ______________________________

❑ Password/hint ______________________________

____

Password/hint change ______________________________

____

____

❑ ✔ if password/PIN are recorded in a separate location

My digital life

General

WEBSITE OR DIGITAL ASSET

❑ website ❑ photo/video/music storage ❑ social media ❑ other

Name of site/asset ______

Website address ______

______

Username/Login ______

______

PIN or Code ______

❑ Password/hint ______

______

Password/hint change ______

______

______

❑ ✔ if password/PIN are recorded in a separate location

WEBSITE OR DIGITAL ASSET

❑ website ❑ photo/video/music storage ❑ social media ❑ other

Name of site/asset ______

Website address ______

______

Username/Login ______

______

PIN or Code ______

❑ Password/hint ______

______

Password/hint change ______

______

______

❑ ✔ if password/PIN are recorded in a separate location

WEBSITE OR DIGITAL ASSET

❑ website ❑ photo/video/music storage ❑ social media ❑ other

Name of site/asset ______________________________

Website address ______________________________

____

Username/Login ______________________________

____

PIN or Code ______________________________

❑ Password/hint ______________________________

____

Password/hint change ______________________________

____

____

❑ ✔ if password/PIN are recorded in a separate location

WEBSITE OR DIGITAL ASSET

❑ website ❑ photo/video/music storage ❑ social media ❑ other

Name of site/asset ______________________________

Website address ______________________________

____

Username/Login ______________________________

____

PIN or Code ______________________________

❑ Password/hint ______________________________

____

Password/hint change ______________________________

____

____

❑ ✔ if password/PIN are recorded in a separate location

My digital life

General

WEBSITE OR DIGITAL ASSET

❑ website ❑ photo/video/music storage ❑ social media ❑ other

Name of site/asset

Website address

Username/Login

PIN or Code

❑ Password/hint

Password/hint change

❑ ✔ if password/PIN are recorded in a separate location

WEBSITE OR DIGITAL ASSET

❑ website ❑ photo/video/music storage ❑ social media ❑ other

Name of site/asset

Website address

Username/Login

PIN or Code

❑ Password/hint

Password/hint change

❑ ✔ if password/PIN are recorded in a separate location

WEBSITE OR DIGITAL ASSET

❑ website ❑ photo/video/music storage ❑ social media ❑ other

Name of site/asset ______________________

Website address ______________________

____

Username/Login ______________________

____

PIN or Code ______________________

❑ Password/hint ______________________

____

Password/hint change ______________________

____

____

❑ ✔ if password/PIN are recorded in a separate location

WEBSITE OR DIGITAL ASSET

❑ website ❑ photo/video/music storage ❑ social media ❑ other

Name of site/asset ______________________

Website address ______________________

____

Username/Login ______________________

____

PIN or Code ______________________

❑ Password/hint ______________________

____

Password/hint change ______________________

____

____

❑ ✔ if password/PIN are recorded in a separate location

My digital life

General

WEBSITE OR DIGITAL ASSET

❑ website ❑ photo/video/music storage ❑ social media ❑ other

Name of site/asset ______

Website address ______

______

Username/Login ______

______

PIN or Code ______

❑ Password/hint ______

______

Password/hint change ______

______

______

❑ ✔ if password/PIN are recorded in a separate location

WEBSITE OR DIGITAL ASSET

❑ website ❑ photo/video/music storage ❑ social media ❑ other

Name of site/asset ______

Website address ______

______

Username/Login ______

______

PIN or Code ______

❑ Password/hint ______

______

Password/hint change ______

______

______

❑ ✔ if password/PIN are recorded in a separate location

WEBSITE OR DIGITAL ASSET

❑ website ❑ photo/video/music storage ❑ social media ❑ other

Name of site/asset ______________________

Website address ______________________

____

Username/Login ______________________

____

PIN or Code ______________________

❑ Password/hint ______________________

____

Password/hint change ______________________

____

____

❑ ✔ if password/PIN are recorded in a separate location

WEBSITE OR DIGITAL ASSET

❑ website ❑ photo/video/music storage ❑ social media ❑ other

Name of site/asset ______________________

Website address ______________________

____

Username/Login ______________________

____

PIN or Code ______________________

❑ Password/hint ______________________

____

Password/hint change ______________________

____

____

❑ ✔ if password/PIN are recorded in a separate location

My digital life

General

WEBSITE OR DIGITAL ASSET

❑ website ❑ photo/video/music storage ❑ social media ❑ other

Name of site/asset ____________________

Website address ____________________

____

Username/Login ____________________

____

PIN or Code ____________________

❑ Password/hint ____________________

____

Password/hint change ____________________

____

____

❑ ✔ if password/PIN are recorded in a separate location

WEBSITE OR DIGITAL ASSET

❑ website ❑ photo/video/music storage ❑ social media ❑ other

Name of site/asset ____________________

Website address ____________________

____

Username/Login ____________________

____

PIN or Code ____________________

❑ Password/hint ____________________

____

Password/hint change ____________________

____

____

❑ ✔ if password/PIN are recorded in a separate location

WEBSITE OR DIGITAL ASSET

❑ website ❑ photo/video/music storage ❑ social media ❑ other

Name of site/asset ______________________

Website address ______________________

____

Username/Login ______________________

____

PIN or Code ______________________

❑ Password/hint ______________________

____

Password/hint change ______________________

____

____

❑ ✔ if password/PIN are recorded in a separate location

WEBSITE OR DIGITAL ASSET

❑ website ❑ photo/video/music storage ❑ social media ❑ other

Name of site/asset ______________________

Website address ______________________

____

Username/Login ______________________

____

PIN or Code ______________________

❑ Password/hint ______________________

____

Password/hint change ______________________

____

____

❑ ✔ if password/PIN are recorded in a separate location

My digital life

General

WEBSITE OR DIGITAL ASSET

❑ website ❑ photo/video/music storage ❑ social media ❑ other

Name of site/asset ______________________

Website address ______________________

____

Username/Login ______________________

____

PIN or Code ______________________

❑ Password/hint ______________________

____

Password/hint change ______________________

____

____

❑ ✔ if password/PIN are recorded in a separate location

WEBSITE OR DIGITAL ASSET

❑ website ❑ photo/video/music storage ❑ social media ❑ other

Name of site/asset ______________________

Website address ______________________

____

Username/Login ______________________

____

PIN or Code ______________________

❑ Password/hint ______________________

____

Password/hint change ______________________

____

____

❑ ✔ if password/PIN are recorded in a separate location

WEBSITE OR DIGITAL ASSET

❑ website ❑ photo/video/music storage ❑ social media ❑ other

Name of site/asset ______________________

Website address ______________________

____

Username/Login ______________________

____

PIN or Code ______________________

❑ Password/hint ______________________

____

Password/hint change ______________________

____

____

❑ ✔ if password/PIN are recorded in a separate location

WEBSITE OR DIGITAL ASSET

❑ website ❑ photo/video/music storage ❑ social media ❑ other

Name of site/asset ______________________

Website address ______________________

____

Username/Login ______________________

____

PIN or Code ______________________

❑ Password/hint ______________________

____

Password/hint change ______________________

____

____

❑ ✔ if password/PIN are recorded in a separate location

My digital life

General

WEBSITE OR DIGITAL ASSET

❑ website ❑ photo/video/music storage ❑ social media ❑ other

Name of site/asset ______________________

Website address ______________________

____

Username/Login ______________________

____

PIN or Code ______________________

❑ Password/hint ______________________

____

Password/hint change ______________________

____

____

❑ ✔ if password/PIN are recorded in a separate location

WEBSITE OR DIGITAL ASSET

❑ website ❑ photo/video/music storage ❑ social media ❑ other

Name of site/asset ______________________

Website address ______________________

____

Username/Login ______________________

____

PIN or Code ______________________

❑ Password/hint ______________________

____

Password/hint change ______________________

____

____

❑ ✔ if password/PIN are recorded in a separate location

WEBSITE OR DIGITAL ASSET

❑ website ❑ photo/video/music storage ❑ social media ❑ other

Name of site/asset ______________________

Website address ______________________

____

Username/Login ______________________

____

PIN or Code ______________________

❑ Password/hint ______________________

____

Password/hint change ______________________

____

____

❑ ✔ if password/PIN are recorded in a separate location

WEBSITE OR DIGITAL ASSET

❑ website ❑ photo/video/music storage ❑ social media ❑ other

Name of site/asset ______________________

Website address ______________________

____

Username/Login ______________________

____

PIN or Code ______________________

❑ Password/hint ______________________

____

Password/hint change ______________________

____

____

❑ ✔ if password/PIN are recorded in a separate location

My digital life

General

WEBSITE OR DIGITAL ASSET

❑ website ❑ photo/video/music storage ❑ social media ❑ other

Name of site/asset ____________________

Website address ____________________

____

Username/Login ____________________

____

PIN or Code ____________________

❑ Password/hint ____________________

____

Password/hint change ____________________

____

____

❑ ✔ if password/PIN are recorded in a separate location

WEBSITE OR DIGITAL ASSET

❑ website ❑ photo/video/music storage ❑ social media ❑ other

Name of site/asset ____________________

Website address ____________________

____

Username/Login ____________________

____

PIN or Code ____________________

❑ Password/hint ____________________

____

Password/hint change ____________________

____

____

❑ ✔ if password/PIN are recorded in a separate location

WEBSITE OR DIGITAL ASSET

❑ website ❑ photo/video/music storage ❑ social media ❑ other

Name of site/asset ______________________

Website address ______________________

____

Username/Login ______________________

____

PIN or Code ______________________

❑ Password/hint ______________________

____

Password/hint change ______________________

____

____

❑ ✔ if password/PIN are recorded in a separate location

WEBSITE OR DIGITAL ASSET

❑ website ❑ photo/video/music storage ❑ social media ❑ other

Name of site/asset ______________________

Website address ______________________

____

Username/Login ______________________

____

PIN or Code ______________________

❑ Password/hint ______________________

____

Password/hint change ______________________

____

____

❑ ✔ if password/PIN are recorded in a separate location

My digital life

General

WEBSITE OR DIGITAL ASSET

❑ website ❑ photo/video/music storage ❑ social media ❑ other

Name of site/asset ______

Website address ______

______

Username/Login ______

______

PIN or Code ______

❑ Password/hint ______

______

Password/hint change ______

______

______

❑ ✔ if password/PIN are recorded in a separate location

WEBSITE OR DIGITAL ASSET

❑ website ❑ photo/video/music storage ❑ social media ❑ other

Name of site/asset ______

Website address ______

______

Username/Login ______

______

PIN or Code ______

❑ Password/hint ______

______

Password/hint change ______

______

______

❑ ✔ if password/PIN are recorded in a separate location

WEBSITE OR DIGITAL ASSET

❑ website ❑ photo/video/music storage ❑ social media ❑ other

Name of site/asset ______________________________

Website address ______________________________

____

Username/Login ______________________________

____

PIN or Code ______________________________

❑ Password/hint ______________________________

____

Password/hint change ______________________________

____

____

❑ ✔ if password/PIN are recorded in a separate location

WEBSITE OR DIGITAL ASSET

❑ website ❑ photo/video/music storage ❑ social media ❑ other

Name of site/asset ______________________________

Website address ______________________________

____

Username/Login ______________________________

____

PIN or Code ______________________________

❑ Password/hint ______________________________

____

Password/hint change ______________________________

____

____

❑ ✔ if password/PIN are recorded in a separate location

My digital life

General

WEBSITE OR DIGITAL ASSET

❑ website ❑ photo/video/music storage ❑ social media ❑ other

Name of site/asset

Website address

Username/Login

PIN or Code

❑ Password/hint

Password/hint change

❑ ✔ if password/PIN are recorded in a separate location

WEBSITE OR DIGITAL ASSET

❑ website ❑ photo/video/music storage ❑ social media ❑ other

Name of site/asset

Website address

Username/Login

PIN or Code

❑ Password/hint

Password/hint change

❑ ✔ if password/PIN are recorded in a separate location

WEBSITE OR DIGITAL ASSET

❑ website ❑ photo/video/music storage ❑ social media ❑ other

Name of site/asset ______________________________

Website address ______________________________

____

Username/Login ______________________________

____

PIN or Code ______________________________

❑ Password/hint ______________________________

____

Password/hint change ______________________________

____

____

❑ ✔ if password/PIN are recorded in a separate location

WEBSITE OR DIGITAL ASSET

❑ website ❑ photo/video/music storage ❑ social media ❑ other

Name of site/asset ______________________________

Website address ______________________________

____

Username/Login ______________________________

____

PIN or Code ______________________________

❑ Password/hint ______________________________

____

Password/hint change ______________________________

____

____

❑ ✔ if password/PIN are recorded in a separate location

My digital life

General

WEBSITE OR DIGITAL ASSET

❑ website ❑ photo/video/music storage ❑ social media ❑ other

Name of site/asset ____________________

Website address ____________________

Username/Login ____________________

PIN or Code ____________________

❑ Password/hint ____________________

Password/hint change ____________________

❑ ✔ if password/PIN are recorded in a separate location

WEBSITE OR DIGITAL ASSET

❑ website ❑ photo/video/music storage ❑ social media ❑ other

Name of site/asset ____________________

Website address ____________________

Username/Login ____________________

PIN or Code ____________________

❑ Password/hint ____________________

Password/hint change ____________________

❑ ✔ if password/PIN are recorded in a separate location

WEBSITE OR DIGITAL ASSET

❑ website ❑ photo/video/music storage ❑ social media ❑ other

Name of site/asset ______________________

Website address ______________________

____

Username/Login ______________________

____

PIN or Code ______________________

❑ Password/hint ______________________

____

Password/hint change ______________________

____

____

❑ ✔ if password/PIN are recorded in a separate location

WEBSITE OR DIGITAL ASSET

❑ website ❑ photo/video/music storage ❑ social media ❑ other

Name of site/asset ______________________

Website address ______________________

____

Username/Login ______________________

____

PIN or Code ______________________

❑ Password/hint ______________________

____

Password/hint change ______________________

____

____

❑ ✔ if password/PIN are recorded in a separate location

My digital life

General

WEBSITE OR DIGITAL ASSET

❑ website ❑ photo/video/music storage ❑ social media ❑ other

Name of site/asset ______

Website address ______

______

Username/Login ______

______

PIN or Code ______

❑ Password/hint ______

______

Password/hint change ______

______

______

❑ ✔ if password/PIN are recorded in a separate location

WEBSITE OR DIGITAL ASSET

❑ website ❑ photo/video/music storage ❑ social media ❑ other

Name of site/asset ______

Website address ______

______

Username/Login ______

______

PIN or Code ______

❑ Password/hint ______

______

Password/hint change ______

______

______

❑ ✔ if password/PIN are recorded in a separate location

WEBSITE OR DIGITAL ASSET

❑ website ❑ photo/video/music storage ❑ social media ❑ other

Name of site/asset ________________

Website address ________________

____

Username/Login ________________

____

PIN or Code ________________

❑ Password/hint ________________

____

Password/hint change ________________

____

____

❑ ✔ if password/PIN are recorded in a separate location

WEBSITE OR DIGITAL ASSET

❑ website ❑ photo/video/music storage ❑ social media ❑ other

Name of site/asset ________________

Website address ________________

____

Username/Login ________________

____

PIN or Code ________________

❑ Password/hint ________________

____

Password/hint change ________________

____

____

❑ ✔ if password/PIN are recorded in a separate location

My digital life

General

WEBSITE OR DIGITAL ASSET

❑ website ❑ photo/video/music storage ❑ social media ❑ other

Name of site/asset ______

Website address ______

______

Username/Login ______

______

PIN or Code ______

❑ Password/hint ______

______

Password/hint change ______

______

______

❑ ✔ if password/PIN are recorded in a separate location

WEBSITE OR DIGITAL ASSET

❑ website ❑ photo/video/music storage ❑ social media ❑ other

Name of site/asset ______

Website address ______

______

Username/Login ______

______

PIN or Code ______

❑ Password/hint ______

______

Password/hint change ______

______

______

❑ ✔ if password/PIN are recorded in a separate location

WEBSITE OR DIGITAL ASSET

❑ website ❑ photo/video/music storage ❑ social media ❑ other

Name of site/asset ______________________

Website address ______________________

____

Username/Login ______________________

____

PIN or Code ______________________

❑ Password/hint ______________________

____

Password/hint change ______________________

____

____

❑ ✔ if password/PIN are recorded in a separate location

WEBSITE OR DIGITAL ASSET

❑ website ❑ photo/video/music storage ❑ social media ❑ other

Name of site/asset ______________________

Website address ______________________

____

Username/Login ______________________

____

PIN or Code ______________________

❑ Password/hint ______________________

____

Password/hint change ______________________

____

____

❑ ✔ if password/PIN are recorded in a separate location

My digital life

General

WEBSITE OR DIGITAL ASSET

❑ website ❑ photo/video/music storage ❑ social media ❑ other

Name of site/asset

Website address

Username/Login

PIN or Code

❑ Password/hint

Password/hint change

❑ ✔ if password/PIN are recorded in a separate location

WEBSITE OR DIGITAL ASSET

❑ website ❑ photo/video/music storage ❑ social media ❑ other

Name of site/asset

Website address

Username/Login

PIN or Code

❑ Password/hint

Password/hint change

❑ ✔ if password/PIN are recorded in a separate location

M

WEBSITE OR DIGITAL ASSET

❑ website ❑ photo/video/music storage ❑ social media ❑ other

Name of site/asset ______________________________

Website address ______________________________

____

Username/Login ______________________________

____

PIN or Code ______________________________

❑ Password/hint ______________________________

____

Password/hint change ______________________________

____

____

❑ ✔ if password/PIN are recorded in a separate location

WEBSITE OR DIGITAL ASSET

❑ website ❑ photo/video/music storage ❑ social media ❑ other

Name of site/asset ______________________________

Website address ______________________________

____

Username/Login ______________________________

____

PIN or Code ______________________________

❑ Password/hint ______________________________

____

Password/hint change ______________________________

____

____

❑ ✔ if password/PIN are recorded in a separate location

My digital life

General

WEBSITE OR DIGITAL ASSET

❑ website ❑ photo/video/music storage ❑ social media ❑ other

Name of site/asset ______________________

Website address ______________________

____

Username/Login ______________________

____

PIN or Code ______________________

❑ Password/hint ______________________

____

Password/hint change ______________________

____

____

❑ ✔ if password/PIN are recorded in a separate location

WEBSITE OR DIGITAL ASSET

❑ website ❑ photo/video/music storage ❑ social media ❑ other

Name of site/asset ______________________

Website address ______________________

____

Username/Login ______________________

____

PIN or Code ______________________

❑ Password/hint ______________________

____

Password/hint change ______________________

____

____

❑ ✔ if password/PIN are recorded in a separate location

WEBSITE OR DIGITAL ASSET

❑ website ❑ photo/video/music storage ❑ social media ❑ other

Name of site/asset ______________________________

Website address ______________________________

____

Username/Login ______________________________

____

PIN or Code ______________________________

❑ Password/hint ______________________________

____

Password/hint change ______________________________

____

____

❑ ✔ if password/PIN are recorded in a separate location

WEBSITE OR DIGITAL ASSET

❑ website ❑ photo/video/music storage ❑ social media ❑ other

Name of site/asset ______________________________

Website address ______________________________

____

Username/Login ______________________________

____

PIN or Code ______________________________

❑ Password/hint ______________________________

____

Password/hint change ______________________________

____

____

❑ ✔ if password/PIN are recorded in a separate location

My digital life

General

WEBSITE OR DIGITAL ASSET

❑ website ❑ photo/video/music storage ❑ social media ❑ other

Name of site/asset ______________________

Website address ______________________

____

Username/Login ______________________

____

PIN or Code ______________________

❑ Password/hint ______________________

____

Password/hint change ______________________

____

____

❑ ✔ if password/PIN are recorded in a separate location

WEBSITE OR DIGITAL ASSET

❑ website ❑ photo/video/music storage ❑ social media ❑ other

Name of site/asset ______________________

Website address ______________________

____

Username/Login ______________________

____

PIN or Code ______________________

❑ Password/hint ______________________

____

Password/hint change ______________________

____

____

❑ ✔ if password/PIN are recorded in a separate location

M

WEBSITE OR DIGITAL ASSET

❑ website ❑ photo/video/music storage ❑ social media ❑ other

Name of site/asset ______________________________

Website address ______________________________

____

Username/Login ______________________________

____

PIN or Code ______________________________

❑ Password/hint ______________________________

____

Password/hint change ______________________________

____

____

❑ ✔ if password/PIN are recorded in a separate location

WEBSITE OR DIGITAL ASSET

❑ website ❑ photo/video/music storage ❑ social media ❑ other

Name of site/asset ______________________________

Website address ______________________________

____

Username/Login ______________________________

____

PIN or Code ______________________________

❑ Password/hint ______________________________

____

Password/hint change ______________________________

____

____

❑ ✔ if password/PIN are recorded in a separate location

My digital life

General

WEBSITE OR DIGITAL ASSET

❑ website ❑ photo/video/music storage ❑ social media ❑ other

Name of site/asset

Website address

Username/Login

PIN or Code

❑ Password/hint

Password/hint change

❑ ✔ if password/PIN are recorded in a separate location

WEBSITE OR DIGITAL ASSET

❑ website ❑ photo/video/music storage ❑ social media ❑ other

Name of site/asset

Website address

Username/Login

PIN or Code

❑ Password/hint

Password/hint change

❑ ✔ if password/PIN are recorded in a separate location

WEBSITE OR DIGITAL ASSET

❑ website ❑ photo/video/music storage ❑ social media ❑ other

Name of site/asset ______________________

Website address ______________________

____

Username/Login ______________________

____

PIN or Code ______________________

❑ Password/hint ______________________

____

Password/hint change ______________________

____

____

❑ ✔ if password/PIN are recorded in a separate location

WEBSITE OR DIGITAL ASSET

❑ website ❑ photo/video/music storage ❑ social media ❑ other

Name of site/asset ______________________

Website address ______________________

____

Username/Login ______________________

____

PIN or Code ______________________

❑ Password/hint ______________________

____

Password/hint change ______________________

____

____

❑ ✔ if password/PIN are recorded in a separate location

WEBSITE OR DIGITAL ASSET

❏ website ❏ photo/video/music storage ❏ social media ❏ other

Name of site/asset ______________________

Website address ______________________

____

Username/Login ______________________

____

PIN or Code ______________________

❏ Password/hint ______________________

____

Password/hint change ______________________

____

____

❏ ✔ if password/PIN are recorded in a separate location

WEBSITE OR DIGITAL ASSET

❏ website ❏ photo/video/music storage ❏ social media ❏ other

Name of site/asset ______________________

Website address ______________________

____

Username/Login ______________________

____

PIN or Code ______________________

❏ Password/hint ______________________

____

Password/hint change ______________________

____

____

❏ ✔ if password/PIN are recorded in a separate location

WEBSITE OR DIGITAL ASSET

❑ website ❑ photo/video/music storage ❑ social media ❑ other

Name of site/asset ______________________

Website address ______________________

____

Username/Login ______________________

____

PIN or Code ______________________

❑ Password/hint ______________________

____

Password/hint change ______________________

____

____

❑ ✔ if password/PIN are recorded in a separate location

WEBSITE OR DIGITAL ASSET

❑ website ❑ photo/video/music storage ❑ social media ❑ other

Name of site/asset ______________________

Website address ______________________

____

Username/Login ______________________

____

PIN or Code ______________________

❑ Password/hint ______________________

____

Password/hint change ______________________

____

____

❑ ✔ if password/PIN are recorded in a separate location

My digital life

General

WEBSITE OR DIGITAL ASSET

❑ website ❑ photo/video/music storage ❑ social media ❑ other

Name of site/asset ______

Website address ______

______

Username/Login ______

______

PIN or Code ______

❑ Password/hint ______

______

Password/hint change ______

______

______

❑ ✔ if password/PIN are recorded in a separate location

WEBSITE OR DIGITAL ASSET

❑ website ❑ photo/video/music storage ❑ social media ❑ other

Name of site/asset ______

Website address ______

______

Username/Login ______

______

PIN or Code ______

❑ Password/hint ______

______

Password/hint change ______

______

______

❑ ✔ if password/PIN are recorded in a separate location

WEBSITE OR DIGITAL ASSET

❑ website ❑ photo/video/music storage ❑ social media ❑ other

Name of site/asset ______________________________

Website address ______________________________

____

Username/Login ______________________________

____

PIN or Code ______________________________

❑ Password/hint ______________________________

____

Password/hint change ______________________________

____

____

❑ ✔ if password/PIN are recorded in a separate location

WEBSITE OR DIGITAL ASSET

❑ website ❑ photo/video/music storage ❑ social media ❑ other

Name of site/asset ______________________________

Website address ______________________________

____

Username/Login ______________________________

____

PIN or Code ______________________________

❑ Password/hint ______________________________

____

Password/hint change ______________________________

____

____

❑ ✔ if password/PIN are recorded in a separate location

My digital life

General

WEBSITE OR DIGITAL ASSET

❑ website ❑ photo/video/music storage ❑ social media ❑ other

Name of site/asset ______

Website address ______

______

Username/Login ______

______

PIN or Code ______

❑ Password/hint ______

______

Password/hint change ______

______

______

❑ ✔ if password/PIN are recorded in a separate location

WEBSITE OR DIGITAL ASSET

❑ website ❑ photo/video/music storage ❑ social media ❑ other

Name of site/asset ______

Website address ______

______

Username/Login ______

______

PIN or Code ______

❑ Password/hint ______

______

Password/hint change ______

______

______

❑ ✔ if password/PIN are recorded in a separate location

WEBSITE OR DIGITAL ASSET

❑ website ❑ photo/video/music storage ❑ social media ❑ other

Name of site/asset ______________________

Website address ______________________

____

Username/Login ______________________

____

PIN or Code ______________________

❑ Password/hint ______________________

____

Password/hint change ______________________

____

____

❑ ✔ if password/PIN are recorded in a separate location

WEBSITE OR DIGITAL ASSET

❑ website ❑ photo/video/music storage ❑ social media ❑ other

Name of site/asset ______________________

Website address ______________________

____

Username/Login ______________________

____

PIN or Code ______________________

❑ Password/hint ______________________

____

Password/hint change ______________________

____

____

❑ ✔ if password/PIN are recorded in a separate location

My digital life

General

WEBSITE OR DIGITAL ASSET

❑ website ❑ photo/video/music storage ❑ social media ❑ other

Name of site/asset ______

Website address ______

______

Username/Login ______

______

PIN or Code ______

❑ Password/hint ______

______

Password/hint change ______

______

______

❑ ✔ if password/PIN are recorded in a separate location

WEBSITE OR DIGITAL ASSET

❑ website ❑ photo/video/music storage ❑ social media ❑ other

Name of site/asset ______

Website address ______

______

Username/Login ______

______

PIN or Code ______

❑ Password/hint ______

______

Password/hint change ______

______

______

❑ ✔ if password/PIN are recorded in a separate location

O

WEBSITE OR DIGITAL ASSET

❑ website ❑ photo/video/music storage ❑ social media ❑ other

Name of site/asset ______________________________

Website address ______________________________

____

Username/Login ______________________________

____

PIN or Code ______________________________

❑ Password/hint ______________________________

____

Password/hint change ______________________________

____

____

❑ ✔ if password/PIN are recorded in a separate location

WEBSITE OR DIGITAL ASSET

❑ website ❑ photo/video/music storage ❑ social media ❑ other

Name of site/asset ______________________________

Website address ______________________________

____

Username/Login ______________________________

____

PIN or Code ______________________________

❑ Password/hint ______________________________

____

Password/hint change ______________________________

____

____

❑ ✔ if password/PIN are recorded in a separate location

My digital life

WEBSITE OR DIGITAL ASSET

❑ website ❑ photo/video/music storage ❑ social media ❑ other

Name of site/asset ______________________

Website address ______________________

____

Username/Login ______________________

____

PIN or Code ______________________

❑ Password/hint ______________________

____

Password/hint change ______________________

____

____

❑ ✔ if password/PIN are recorded in a separate location

WEBSITE OR DIGITAL ASSET

❑ website ❑ photo/video/music storage ❑ social media ❑ other

Name of site/asset ______________________

Website address ______________________

____

Username/Login ______________________

____

PIN or Code ______________________

❑ Password/hint ______________________

____

Password/hint change ______________________

____

____

❑ ✔ if password/PIN are recorded in a separate location

WEBSITE OR DIGITAL ASSET

❑ website ❑ photo/video/music storage ❑ social media ❑ other

Name of site/asset ______________________

Website address ______________________

____

Username/Login ______________________

____

PIN or Code ______________________

❑ Password/hint ______________________

____

Password/hint change ______________________

____

____

❑ ✔ if password/PIN are recorded in a separate location

WEBSITE OR DIGITAL ASSET

❑ website ❑ photo/video/music storage ❑ social media ❑ other

Name of site/asset ______________________

Website address ______________________

____

Username/Login ______________________

____

PIN or Code ______________________

❑ Password/hint ______________________

____

Password/hint change ______________________

____

____

❑ ✔ if password/PIN are recorded in a separate location

My digital life

General

WEBSITE OR DIGITAL ASSET

❑ website ❑ photo/video/music storage ❑ social media ❑ other

Name of site/asset ______

Website address ______

______

Username/Login ______

______

PIN or Code ______

❑ Password/hint ______

______

Password/hint change ______

______

______

❑ ✔ if password/PIN are recorded in a separate location

WEBSITE OR DIGITAL ASSET

❑ website ❑ photo/video/music storage ❑ social media ❑ other

Name of site/asset ______

Website address ______

______

Username/Login ______

______

PIN or Code ______

❑ Password/hint ______

______

Password/hint change ______

______

______

❑ ✔ if password/PIN are recorded in a separate location

WEBSITE OR DIGITAL ASSET

❑ website ❑ photo/video/music storage ❑ social media ❑ other

Name of site/asset ______________________

Website address ______________________

____

Username/Login ______________________

____

PIN or Code ______________________

❑ Password/hint ______________________

____

Password/hint change ______________________

____

____

❑ ✔ if password/PIN are recorded in a separate location

WEBSITE OR DIGITAL ASSET

❑ website ❑ photo/video/music storage ❑ social media ❑ other

Name of site/asset ______________________

Website address ______________________

____

Username/Login ______________________

____

PIN or Code ______________________

❑ Password/hint ______________________

____

Password/hint change ______________________

____

____

❑ ✔ if password/PIN are recorded in a separate location

My digital life

WEBSITE OR DIGITAL ASSET

❑ website ❑ photo/video/music storage ❑ social media ❑ other

Name of site/asset ______

Website address ______

______

Username/Login ______

______

PIN or Code ______

❑ Password/hint ______

______

Password/hint change ______

______

______

❑ ✔ if password/PIN are recorded in a separate location

WEBSITE OR DIGITAL ASSET

❑ website ❑ photo/video/music storage ❑ social media ❑ other

Name of site/asset ______

Website address ______

______

Username/Login ______

______

PIN or Code ______

❑ Password/hint ______

______

Password/hint change ______

______

______

❑ ✔ if password/PIN are recorded in a separate location

WEBSITE OR DIGITAL ASSET

❑ website ❑ photo/video/music storage ❑ social media ❑ other

Name of site/asset ______________________

Website address ______________________

____

Username/Login ______________________

____

PIN or Code ______________________

❑ Password/hint ______________________

____

Password/hint change ______________________

____

____

❑ ✔ if password/PIN are recorded in a separate location

WEBSITE OR DIGITAL ASSET

❑ website ❑ photo/video/music storage ❑ social media ❑ other

Name of site/asset ______________________

Website address ______________________

____

Username/Login ______________________

____

PIN or Code ______________________

❑ Password/hint ______________________

____

Password/hint change ______________________

____

____

❑ ✔ if password/PIN are recorded in a separate location

My digital life

General

WEBSITE OR DIGITAL ASSET

❑ website ❑ photo/video/music storage ❑ social media ❑ other

Name of site/asset ____________________

Website address ____________________

____

Username/Login ____________________

____

PIN or Code ____________________

❑ Password/hint ____________________

____

Password/hint change ____________________

____

____

❑ ✔ if password/PIN are recorded in a separate location

WEBSITE OR DIGITAL ASSET

❑ website ❑ photo/video/music storage ❑ social media ❑ other

Name of site/asset ____________________

Website address ____________________

____

Username/Login ____________________

____

PIN or Code ____________________

❑ Password/hint ____________________

____

Password/hint change ____________________

____

____

❑ ✔ if password/PIN are recorded in a separate location

WEBSITE OR DIGITAL ASSET

❑ website ❑ photo/video/music storage ❑ social media ❑ other

Name of site/asset ______________________________

Website address ______________________________

____

Username/Login ______________________________

____

PIN or Code ______________________________

❑ Password/hint ______________________________

____

Password/hint change ______________________________

____

____

❑ ✔ if password/PIN are recorded in a separate location

WEBSITE OR DIGITAL ASSET

❑ website ❑ photo/video/music storage ❑ social media ❑ other

Name of site/asset ______________________________

Website address ______________________________

____

Username/Login ______________________________

____

PIN or Code ______________________________

❑ Password/hint ______________________________

____

Password/hint change ______________________________

____

____

❑ ✔ if password/PIN are recorded in a separate location

My digital life

General

WEBSITE OR DIGITAL ASSET

❑ website ❑ photo/video/music storage ❑ social media ❑ other

Name of site/asset ______________________

Website address ______________________

____

Username/Login ______________________

____

PIN or Code ______________________

❑ Password/hint ______________________

____

Password/hint change ______________________

____

____

❑ ✔ if password/PIN are recorded in a separate location

WEBSITE OR DIGITAL ASSET

❑ website ❑ photo/video/music storage ❑ social media ❑ other

Name of site/asset ______________________

Website address ______________________

____

Username/Login ______________________

____

PIN or Code ______________________

❑ Password/hint ______________________

____

Password/hint change ______________________

____

____

❑ ✔ if password/PIN are recorded in a separate location

WEBSITE OR DIGITAL ASSET

❑ website ❑ photo/video/music storage ❑ social media ❑ other

Name of site/asset

Website address

Username/Login

PIN or Code

❑ Password/hint

Password/hint change

❑ ✔ if password/PIN are recorded in a separate location

WEBSITE OR DIGITAL ASSET

❑ website ❑ photo/video/music storage ❑ social media ❑ other

Name of site/asset

Website address

Username/Login

PIN or Code

❑ Password/hint

Password/hint change

❑ ✔ if password/PIN are recorded in a separate location

My digital life

General

WEBSITE OR DIGITAL ASSET

❑ website ❑ photo/video/music storage ❑ social media ❑ other

Name of site/asset

Website address

Username/Login

PIN or Code

❑ Password/hint

Password/hint change

❑ ✔ if password/PIN are recorded in a separate location

WEBSITE OR DIGITAL ASSET

❑ website ❑ photo/video/music storage ❑ social media ❑ other

Name of site/asset

Website address

Username/Login

PIN or Code

❑ Password/hint

Password/hint change

❑ ✔ if password/PIN are recorded in a separate location

WEBSITE OR DIGITAL ASSET

❑ website ❑ photo/video/music storage ❑ social media ❑ other

Name of site/asset ______________________________

Website address ______________________________

____

Username/Login ______________________________

____

PIN or Code ______________________________

❑ Password/hint ______________________________

____

Password/hint change ______________________________

____

____

❑ ✔ if password/PIN are recorded in a separate location

WEBSITE OR DIGITAL ASSET

❑ website ❑ photo/video/music storage ❑ social media ❑ other

Name of site/asset ______________________________

Website address ______________________________

____

Username/Login ______________________________

____

PIN or Code ______________________________

❑ Password/hint ______________________________

____

Password/hint change ______________________________

____

____

❑ ✔ if password/PIN are recorded in a separate location

My digital life

General

WEBSITE OR DIGITAL ASSET

❑ website ❑ photo/video/music storage ❑ social media ❑ other

Name of site/asset ______________________

Website address ______________________

____

Username/Login ______________________

____

PIN or Code ______________________

❑ Password/hint ______________________

____

Password/hint change ______________________

____

____

❑ ✔ if password/PIN are recorded in a separate location

WEBSITE OR DIGITAL ASSET

❑ website ❑ photo/video/music storage ❑ social media ❑ other

Name of site/asset ______________________

Website address ______________________

____

Username/Login ______________________

____

PIN or Code ______________________

❑ Password/hint ______________________

____

Password/hint change ______________________

____

____

❑ ✔ if password/PIN are recorded in a separate location

WEBSITE OR DIGITAL ASSET

❑ website ❑ photo/video/music storage ❑ social media ❑ other

Name of site/asset ______________________________

Website address ______________________________

____

Username/Login ______________________________

____

PIN or Code ______________________________

❑ Password/hint ______________________________

____

Password/hint change ______________________________

____

____

❑ ✔ if password/PIN are recorded in a separate location

WEBSITE OR DIGITAL ASSET

❑ website ❑ photo/video/music storage ❑ social media ❑ other

Name of site/asset ______________________________

Website address ______________________________

____

Username/Login ______________________________

____

PIN or Code ______________________________

❑ Password/hint ______________________________

____

Password/hint change ______________________________

____

____

❑ ✔ if password/PIN are recorded in a separate location

My digital life

General

WEBSITE OR DIGITAL ASSET

❑ website ❑ photo/video/music storage ❑ social media ❑ other

Name of site/asset ____________________

Website address ____________________

____

Username/Login ____________________

____

PIN or Code ____________________

❑ Password/hint ____________________

____

Password/hint change ____________________

____

____

❑ ✔ if password/PIN are recorded in a separate location

WEBSITE OR DIGITAL ASSET

❑ website ❑ photo/video/music storage ❑ social media ❑ other

Name of site/asset ____________________

Website address ____________________

____

Username/Login ____________________

____

PIN or Code ____________________

❑ Password/hint ____________________

____

Password/hint change ____________________

____

____

❑ ✔ if password/PIN are recorded in a separate location

WEBSITE OR DIGITAL ASSET

❑ website ❑ photo/video/music storage ❑ social media ❑ other

Name of site/asset ______________________________

Website address ______________________________

____

Username/Login ______________________________

____

PIN or Code ______________________________

❑ Password/hint ______________________________

____

Password/hint change ______________________________

____

____

❑ ✔ if password/PIN are recorded in a separate location

WEBSITE OR DIGITAL ASSET

❑ website ❑ photo/video/music storage ❑ social media ❑ other

Name of site/asset ______________________________

Website address ______________________________

____

Username/Login ______________________________

____

PIN or Code ______________________________

❑ Password/hint ______________________________

____

Password/hint change ______________________________

____

____

❑ ✔ if password/PIN are recorded in a separate location

My digital life

General

WEBSITE OR DIGITAL ASSET

❑ website ❑ photo/video/music storage ❑ social media ❑ other

Name of site/asset

Website address

Username/Login

PIN or Code

❑ Password/hint

Password/hint change

❑ ✔ if password/PIN are recorded in a separate location

WEBSITE OR DIGITAL ASSET

❑ website ❑ photo/video/music storage ❑ social media ❑ other

Name of site/asset

Website address

Username/Login

PIN or Code

❑ Password/hint

Password/hint change

❑ ✔ if password/PIN are recorded in a separate location

WEBSITE OR DIGITAL ASSET

❑ website ❑ photo/video/music storage ❑ social media ❑ other

Name of site/asset ______________________

Website address ______________________

____

Username/Login ______________________

____

PIN or Code ______________________

❑ Password/hint ______________________

____

Password/hint change ______________________

____

____

❑ ✔ if password/PIN are recorded in a separate location

WEBSITE OR DIGITAL ASSET

❑ website ❑ photo/video/music storage ❑ social media ❑ other

Name of site/asset ______________________

Website address ______________________

____

Username/Login ______________________

____

PIN or Code ______________________

❑ Password/hint ______________________

____

Password/hint change ______________________

____

____

❑ ✔ if password/PIN are recorded in a separate location

My digital life

General

WEBSITE OR DIGITAL ASSET

❑ website ❑ photo/video/music storage ❑ social media ❑ other

Name of site/asset __________

Website address __________

Username/Login __________

PIN or Code __________

❑ Password/hint __________

Password/hint change __________

❑ ✔ if password/PIN are recorded in a separate location

WEBSITE OR DIGITAL ASSET

❑ website ❑ photo/video/music storage ❑ social media ❑ other

Name of site/asset __________

Website address __________

Username/Login __________

PIN or Code __________

❑ Password/hint __________

Password/hint change __________

❑ ✔ if password/PIN are recorded in a separate location

WEBSITE OR DIGITAL ASSET

❑ website ❑ photo/video/music storage ❑ social media ❑ other

Name of site/asset ______________________

Website address ______________________

____

Username/Login ______________________

____

PIN or Code ______________________

❑ Password/hint ______________________

____

Password/hint change ______________________

____

____

❑ ✔ if password/PIN are recorded in a separate location

WEBSITE OR DIGITAL ASSET

❑ website ❑ photo/video/music storage ❑ social media ❑ other

Name of site/asset ______________________

Website address ______________________

____

Username/Login ______________________

____

PIN or Code ______________________

❑ Password/hint ______________________

____

Password/hint change ______________________

____

____

❑ ✔ if password/PIN are recorded in a separate location

My digital life

General

WEBSITE OR DIGITAL ASSET

❑ website ❑ photo/video/music storage ❑ social media ❑ other

Name of site/asset ______________________

Website address ______________________

____

Username/Login ______________________

____

PIN or Code ______________________

❑ Password/hint ______________________

____

Password/hint change ______________________

____

____

❑ ✔ if password/PIN are recorded in a separate location

WEBSITE OR DIGITAL ASSET

❑ website ❑ photo/video/music storage ❑ social media ❑ other

Name of site/asset ______________________

Website address ______________________

____

Username/Login ______________________

____

PIN or Code ______________________

❑ Password/hint ______________________

____

Password/hint change ______________________

____

____

❑ ✔ if password/PIN are recorded in a separate location

WEBSITE OR DIGITAL ASSET

❑ website ❑ photo/video/music storage ❑ social media ❑ other

Name of site/asset ______________________________

Website address ______________________________

____

Username/Login ______________________________

____

PIN or Code ______________________________

❑ Password/hint ______________________________

____

Password/hint change ______________________________

____

____

❑ ✔ if password/PIN are recorded in a separate location

WEBSITE OR DIGITAL ASSET

❑ website ❑ photo/video/music storage ❑ social media ❑ other

Name of site/asset ______________________________

Website address ______________________________

____

Username/Login ______________________________

____

PIN or Code ______________________________

❑ Password/hint ______________________________

____

Password/hint change ______________________________

____

____

❑ ✔ if password/PIN are recorded in a separate location

My digital life

General

WEBSITE OR DIGITAL ASSET

❑ website ❑ photo/video/music storage ❑ social media ❑ other

Name of site/asset ______

Website address ______

______

Username/Login ______

______

PIN or Code ______

❑ Password/hint ______

______

Password/hint change ______

______

______

❑ ✔ if password/PIN are recorded in a separate location

WEBSITE OR DIGITAL ASSET

❑ website ❑ photo/video/music storage ❑ social media ❑ other

Name of site/asset ______

Website address ______

______

Username/Login ______

______

PIN or Code ______

❑ Password/hint ______

______

Password/hint change ______

______

______

❑ ✔ if password/PIN are recorded in a separate location

WEBSITE OR DIGITAL ASSET

❑ website ❑ photo/video/music storage ❑ social media ❑ other

Name of site/asset ______

Website address ______

______

Username/Login ______

______

PIN or Code ______

❑ Password/hint ______

______

Password/hint change ______

______

______

❑ ✔ if password/PIN are recorded in a separate location

WEBSITE OR DIGITAL ASSET

❑ website ❑ photo/video/music storage ❑ social media ❑ other

Name of site/asset ______

Website address ______

______

Username/Login ______

______

PIN or Code ______

❑ Password/hint ______

______

Password/hint change ______

______

______

❑ ✔ if password/PIN are recorded in a separate location

My digital life

General

WEBSITE OR DIGITAL ASSET

❑ website ❑ photo/video/music storage ❑ social media ❑ other

Name of site/asset ____________________

Website address ____________________

____

Username/Login ____________________

____

PIN or Code ____________________

❑ Password/hint ____________________

____

Password/hint change ____________________

____

____

❑ ✔ if password/PIN are recorded in a separate location

WEBSITE OR DIGITAL ASSET

❑ website ❑ photo/video/music storage ❑ social media ❑ other

Name of site/asset ____________________

Website address ____________________

____

Username/Login ____________________

____

PIN or Code ____________________

❑ Password/hint ____________________

____

Password/hint change ____________________

____

____

❑ ✔ if password/PIN are recorded in a separate location

WEBSITE OR DIGITAL ASSET

❑ website ❑ photo/video/music storage ❑ social media ❑ other

Name of site/asset ______________________

Website address ______________________

____

Username/Login ______________________

____

PIN or Code ______________________

❑ Password/hint ______________________

____

Password/hint change ______________________

____

____

❑ ✔ if password/PIN are recorded in a separate location

WEBSITE OR DIGITAL ASSET

❑ website ❑ photo/video/music storage ❑ social media ❑ other

Name of site/asset ______________________

Website address ______________________

____

Username/Login ______________________

____

PIN or Code ______________________

❑ Password/hint ______________________

____

Password/hint change ______________________

____

____

❑ ✔ if password/PIN are recorded in a separate location

My digital life

General

WEBSITE OR DIGITAL ASSET

❑ website ❑ photo/video/music storage ❑ social media ❑ other

Name of site/asset ______________________

Website address ______________________

____

Username/Login ______________________

____

PIN or Code ______________________

❑ Password/hint ______________________

____

Password/hint change ______________________

____

____

❑ ✔ if password/PIN are recorded in a separate location

WEBSITE OR DIGITAL ASSET

❑ website ❑ photo/video/music storage ❑ social media ❑ other

Name of site/asset ______________________

Website address ______________________

____

Username/Login ______________________

____

PIN or Code ______________________

❑ Password/hint ______________________

____

Password/hint change ______________________

____

____

❑ ✔ if password/PIN are recorded in a separate location

T

WEBSITE OR DIGITAL ASSET

❑ website ❑ photo/video/music storage ❑ social media ❑ other

Name of site/asset ______________________

Website address ______________________

____

Username/Login ______________________

____

PIN or Code ______________________

❑ Password/hint ______________________

____

Password/hint change ______________________

____

____

❑ ✔ if password/PIN are recorded in a separate location

WEBSITE OR DIGITAL ASSET

❑ website ❑ photo/video/music storage ❑ social media ❑ other

Name of site/asset ______________________

Website address ______________________

____

Username/Login ______________________

____

PIN or Code ______________________

❑ Password/hint ______________________

____

Password/hint change ______________________

____

____

❑ ✔ if password/PIN are recorded in a separate location

My digital life

General

WEBSITE OR DIGITAL ASSET

❑ website ❑ photo/video/music storage ❑ social media ❑ other

Name of site/asset ______

Website address ______

______

Username/Login ______

______

PIN or Code ______

❑ Password/hint ______

______

Password/hint change ______

______

______

❑ ✔ if password/PIN are recorded in a separate location

WEBSITE OR DIGITAL ASSET

❑ website ❑ photo/video/music storage ❑ social media ❑ other

Name of site/asset ______

Website address ______

______

Username/Login ______

______

PIN or Code ______

❑ Password/hint ______

______

Password/hint change ______

______

______

❑ ✔ if password/PIN are recorded in a separate location

WEBSITE OR DIGITAL ASSET

❑ website ❑ photo/video/music storage ❑ social media ❑ other

Name of site/asset ______________________

Website address ______________________

____

Username/Login ______________________

____

PIN or Code ______________________

❑ Password/hint ______________________

____

Password/hint change ______________________

____

____

❑ ✔ if password/PIN are recorded in a separate location

WEBSITE OR DIGITAL ASSET

❑ website ❑ photo/video/music storage ❑ social media ❑ other

Name of site/asset ______________________

Website address ______________________

____

Username/Login ______________________

____

PIN or Code ______________________

❑ Password/hint ______________________

____

Password/hint change ______________________

____

____

❑ ✔ if password/PIN are recorded in a separate location

My digital life

General

WEBSITE OR DIGITAL ASSET

❑ website ❑ photo/video/music storage ❑ social media ❑ other

Name of site/asset ______

Website address ______

______

Username/Login ______

______

PIN or Code ______

❑ Password/hint ______

______

Password/hint change ______

______

______

❑ ✔ if password/PIN are recorded in a separate location

WEBSITE OR DIGITAL ASSET

❑ website ❑ photo/video/music storage ❑ social media ❑ other

Name of site/asset ______

Website address ______

______

Username/Login ______

______

PIN or Code ______

❑ Password/hint ______

______

Password/hint change ______

______

______

❑ ✔ if password/PIN are recorded in a separate location

WEBSITE OR DIGITAL ASSET

❑ website ❑ photo/video/music storage ❑ social media ❑ other

Name of site/asset ______________________

Website address ______________________

____

Username/Login ______________________

____

PIN or Code ______________________

❑ Password/hint ______________________

____

Password/hint change ______________________

____

____

❑ ✔ if password/PIN are recorded in a separate location

WEBSITE OR DIGITAL ASSET

❑ website ❑ photo/video/music storage ❑ social media ❑ other

Name of site/asset ______________________

Website address ______________________

____

Username/Login ______________________

____

PIN or Code ______________________

❑ Password/hint ______________________

____

Password/hint change ______________________

____

____

❑ ✔ if password/PIN are recorded in a separate location

My digital life

General

WEBSITE OR DIGITAL ASSET

❑ website ❑ photo/video/music storage ❑ social media ❑ other

Name of site/asset ______________________

Website address ______________________

____

Username/Login ______________________

____

PIN or Code ______________________

❑ Password/hint ______________________

____

Password/hint change ______________________

____

____

❑ ✔ if password/PIN are recorded in a separate location

WEBSITE OR DIGITAL ASSET

❑ website ❑ photo/video/music storage ❑ social media ❑ other

Name of site/asset ______________________

Website address ______________________

____

Username/Login ______________________

____

PIN or Code ______________________

❑ Password/hint ______________________

____

Password/hint change ______________________

____

____

❑ ✔ if password/PIN are recorded in a separate location

WEBSITE OR DIGITAL ASSET

❑ website ❑ photo/video/music storage ❑ social media ❑ other

Name of site/asset ______________________________

Website address ______________________________

____

Username/Login ______________________________

____

PIN or Code ______________________________

❑ Password/hint ______________________________

____

Password/hint change ______________________________

____

____

❑ ✔ if password/PIN are recorded in a separate location

WEBSITE OR DIGITAL ASSET

❑ website ❑ photo/video/music storage ❑ social media ❑ other

Name of site/asset ______________________________

Website address ______________________________

____

Username/Login ______________________________

____

PIN or Code ______________________________

❑ Password/hint ______________________________

____

Password/hint change ______________________________

____

____

❑ ✔ if password/PIN are recorded in a separate location

My digital life

General

WEBSITE OR DIGITAL ASSET

❑ website ❑ photo/video/music storage ❑ social media ❑ other

Name of site/asset ______________________

Website address ______________________

____

Username/Login ______________________

____

PIN or Code ______________________

❑ Password/hint ______________________

____

Password/hint change ______________________

____

____

❑ ✔ if password/PIN are recorded in a separate location

WEBSITE OR DIGITAL ASSET

❑ website ❑ photo/video/music storage ❑ social media ❑ other

Name of site/asset ______________________

Website address ______________________

____

Username/Login ______________________

____

PIN or Code ______________________

❑ Password/hint ______________________

____

Password/hint change ______________________

____

____

❑ ✔ if password/PIN are recorded in a separate location

WEBSITE OR DIGITAL ASSET

❑ website ❑ photo/video/music storage ❑ social media ❑ other

Name of site/asset ______________________________

Website address ______________________________

____

Username/Login ______________________________

____

PIN or Code ______________________________

❑ Password/hint ______________________________

____

Password/hint change ______________________________

____

____

❑ ✔ if password/PIN are recorded in a separate location

WEBSITE OR DIGITAL ASSET

❑ website ❑ photo/video/music storage ❑ social media ❑ other

Name of site/asset ______________________________

Website address ______________________________

____

Username/Login ______________________________

____

PIN or Code ______________________________

❑ Password/hint ______________________________

____

Password/hint change ______________________________

____

____

❑ ✔ if password/PIN are recorded in a separate location

My digital life

General

WEBSITE OR DIGITAL ASSET

❑ website ❑ photo/video/music storage ❑ social media ❑ other

Name of site/asset ______________________________

Website address ______________________________

____

Username/Login ______________________________

____

PIN or Code ______________________________

❑ Password/hint ______________________________

____

Password/hint change ______________________________

____

____

❑ ✔ if password/PIN are recorded in a separate location

WEBSITE OR DIGITAL ASSET

❑ website ❑ photo/video/music storage ❑ social media ❑ other

Name of site/asset ______________________________

Website address ______________________________

____

Username/Login ______________________________

____

PIN or Code ______________________________

❑ Password/hint ______________________________

____

Password/hint change ______________________________

____

____

❑ ✔ if password/PIN are recorded in a separate location

WEBSITE OR DIGITAL ASSET

❑ website ❑ photo/video/music storage ❑ social media ❑ other

Name of site/asset ______________________

Website address ______________________

____

Username/Login ______________________

____

PIN or Code ______________________

❑ Password/hint ______________________

____

Password/hint change ______________________

____

____

❑ ✔ if password/PIN are recorded in a separate location

WEBSITE OR DIGITAL ASSET

❑ website ❑ photo/video/music storage ❑ social media ❑ other

Name of site/asset ______________________

Website address ______________________

____

Username/Login ______________________

____

PIN or Code ______________________

❑ Password/hint ______________________

____

Password/hint change ______________________

____

____

❑ ✔ if password/PIN are recorded in a separate location

My digital life

General

WEBSITE OR DIGITAL ASSET

❑ website ❑ photo/video/music storage ❑ social media ❑ other

Name of site/asset ______________________

Website address ______________________

____

Username/Login ______________________

____

PIN or Code ______________________

❑ Password/hint ______________________

____

Password/hint change ______________________

____

____

❑ ✔ if password/PIN are recorded in a separate location

WEBSITE OR DIGITAL ASSET

❑ website ❑ photo/video/music storage ❑ social media ❑ other

Name of site/asset ______________________

Website address ______________________

____

Username/Login ______________________

____

PIN or Code ______________________

❑ Password/hint ______________________

____

Password/hint change ______________________

____

____

❑ ✔ if password/PIN are recorded in a separate location

WEBSITE OR DIGITAL ASSET

❑ website ❑ photo/video/music storage ❑ social media ❑ other

Name of site/asset ______________________

Website address ______________________

____

Username/Login ______________________

____

PIN or Code ______________________

❑ Password/hint ______________________

____

Password/hint change ______________________

____

____

❑ ✔ if password/PIN are recorded in a separate location

WEBSITE OR DIGITAL ASSET

❑ website ❑ photo/video/music storage ❑ social media ❑ other

Name of site/asset ______________________

Website address ______________________

____

Username/Login ______________________

____

PIN or Code ______________________

❑ Password/hint ______________________

____

Password/hint change ______________________

____

____

❑ ✔ if password/PIN are recorded in a separate location

My digital life

General

WEBSITE OR DIGITAL ASSET

❑ website ❑ photo/video/music storage ❑ social media ❑ other

Name of site/asset ______________________

Website address ______________________

____

Username/Login ______________________

____

PIN or Code ______________________

❑ Password/hint ______________________

____

Password/hint change ______________________

____

____

❑ ✔ if password/PIN are recorded in a separate location

WEBSITE OR DIGITAL ASSET

❑ website ❑ photo/video/music storage ❑ social media ❑ other

Name of site/asset ______________________

Website address ______________________

____

Username/Login ______________________

____

PIN or Code ______________________

❑ Password/hint ______________________

____

Password/hint change ______________________

____

____

❑ ✔ if password/PIN are recorded in a separate location

WEBSITE OR DIGITAL ASSET

❑ website ❑ photo/video/music storage ❑ social media ❑ other

Name of site/asset ______________________

Website address ______________________

____

Username/Login ______________________

____

PIN or Code ______________________

❑ Password/hint ______________________

____

Password/hint change ______________________

____

____

❑ ✔ if password/PIN are recorded in a separate location

WEBSITE OR DIGITAL ASSET

❑ website ❑ photo/video/music storage ❑ social media ❑ other

Name of site/asset ______________________

Website address ______________________

____

Username/Login ______________________

____

PIN or Code ______________________

❑ Password/hint ______________________

____

Password/hint change ______________________

____

____

❑ ✔ if password/PIN are recorded in a separate location

My digital life

General

WEBSITE OR DIGITAL ASSET

❏ website ❏ photo/video/music storage ❏ social media ❏ other

Name of site/asset ______

Website address ______

______

Username/Login ______

______

PIN or Code ______

❏ Password/hint ______

______

Password/hint change ______

______

______

❏ ✔ if password/PIN are recorded in a separate location

WEBSITE OR DIGITAL ASSET

❏ website ❏ photo/video/music storage ❏ social media ❏ other

Name of site/asset ______

Website address ______

______

Username/Login ______

______

PIN or Code ______

❏ Password/hint ______

______

Password/hint change ______

______

______

❏ ✔ if password/PIN are recorded in a separate location

WEBSITE OR DIGITAL ASSET

❑ website ❑ photo/video/music storage ❑ social media ❑ other

Name of site/asset ______________________________

Website address ______________________________

____

Username/Login ______________________________

____

PIN or Code ______________________________

❑ Password/hint ______________________________

____

Password/hint change ______________________________

____

____

❑ ✔ if password/PIN are recorded in a separate location

WEBSITE OR DIGITAL ASSET

❑ website ❑ photo/video/music storage ❑ social media ❑ other

Name of site/asset ______________________________

Website address ______________________________

____

Username/Login ______________________________

____

PIN or Code ______________________________

❑ Password/hint ______________________________

____

Password/hint change ______________________________

____

____

❑ ✔ if password/PIN are recorded in a separate location

My digital life

General

WEBSITE OR DIGITAL ASSET

❑ website ❑ photo/video/music storage ❑ social media ❑ other

Name of site/asset ______________________________

Website address ______________________________

____

Username/Login ______________________________

____

PIN or Code ______________________________

❑ Password/hint ______________________________

____

Password/hint change ______________________________

____

____

❑ ✔ if password/PIN are recorded in a separate location

WEBSITE OR DIGITAL ASSET

❑ website ❑ photo/video/music storage ❑ social media ❑ other

Name of site/asset ______________________________

Website address ______________________________

____

Username/Login ______________________________

____

PIN or Code ______________________________

❑ Password/hint ______________________________

____

Password/hint change ______________________________

____

____

❑ ✔ if password/PIN are recorded in a separate location

WEBSITE OR DIGITAL ASSET

❑ website ❑ photo/video/music storage ❑ social media ❑ other

Name of site/asset ______

Website address ______

______

Username/Login ______

______

PIN or Code ______

❑ Password/hint ______

______

Password/hint change ______

______

______

❑ ✔ if password/PIN are recorded in a separate location

WEBSITE OR DIGITAL ASSET

❑ website ❑ photo/video/music storage ❑ social media ❑ other

Name of site/asset ______

Website address ______

______

Username/Login ______

______

PIN or Code ______

❑ Password/hint ______

______

Password/hint change ______

______

______

❑ ✔ if password/PIN are recorded in a separate location

Online Accounts I Pay Into or Collect Money From

My digital life $ Affiliate, retail, etc.

TYPE OF ONLINE ACCOUNT

❑ affiliate ❑ online store ❑ membership site ❑ digital storage

❑ service or software subscription ❑ other ______

Name of site/asset ______

Website address ______

______

❑ **This is a site I pay into**

How much do I pay? $ ______

How often do I pay? ______

How do I pay? ______

❑ **This is an income-generating site**

How often do I get paid? ______

How do I get paid? ______

______

Member # ______

STATUS: ❍ Active member ❍ Inactive member ❍ Cancelled

Contact Info ______

Username/Login ______

______

PIN or Code ______

Password/hint ______

______

Password/hint change ______

______

______

______

❑ ✔ if password/PIN are recorded in a separate location

NOTES ______

______

______

TYPE OF ONLINE ACCOUNT

❑ affiliate ❑ online store ❑ membership site ❑ digital storage

❑ service or software subscription ❑ other ____________________

Name of site/asset ____________________

Website address ____________________

____

❑ This is a site I pay into

How much do I pay? $ ____________________

How often do I pay? ____________________

How do I pay? ____________________

❑ This is an income-generating site

How often do I get paid? ____________________

How do I get paid? ____________________

____

Member # ____________________

STATUS: ❍ Active member ❍ Inactive member ❍ Cancelled

Contact Info ____________________

Username/Login ____________________

____

PIN or Code ____________________

Password/hint ____________________

____

Password/hint change ____________________

____

____

____

❑ ✔ if password/PIN are recorded in a separate location

NOTES

____

____

____

____

My digital life $ Affiliate, retail, etc.

TYPE OF ONLINE ACCOUNT

❑ affiliate ❑ online store ❑ membership site ❑ digital storage

❑ service or software subscription ❑ other ______________________

Name of site/asset ______________________

Website address ______________________

____

❑ **This is a site I pay into**

How much do I pay? $ ______________________

How often do I pay? ______________________

How do I pay? ______________________

❑ **This is an income-generating site**

How often do I get paid? ______________________

How do I get paid? ______________________

____

Member # ______________________

STATUS: ❍ Active member ❍ Inactive member ❍ Cancelled

Contact Info ______________________

Username/Login ______________________

____

PIN or Code ______________________

Password/hint ______________________

____

Password/hint change ______________________

____

____

____

❑ ✔ if password/PIN are recorded in a separate location

NOTES ______________________

____

____

TYPE OF ONLINE ACCOUNT

❑ affiliate ❑ online store ❑ membership site ❑ digital storage

❑ service or software subscription ❑ other ______

Name of site/asset ______

Website address ______

______

❑ This is a site I pay into

How much do I pay? $ ______

How often do I pay? ______

How do I pay? ______

❑ This is an income-generating site

How often do I get paid? ______

How do I get paid? ______

______

Member # ______

STATUS: ❍ Active member ❍ Inactive member ❍ Cancelled

Contact Info ______

Username/Login ______

______

PIN or Code ______

Password/hint ______

______

Password/hint change ______

______

______

______

❑ ✔ if password/PIN are recorded in a separate location

NOTES

______

______

______

______

My digital life $ Affiliate, retail, etc.

TYPE OF ONLINE ACCOUNT

❑ affiliate ❑ online store ❑ membership site ❑ digital storage

❑ service or software subscription ❑ other ______

Name of site/asset ______

Website address ______

______

❑ This is a site I pay into

How much do I pay? $ ______

How often do I pay? ______

How do I pay? ______

❑ This is an income-generating site

How often do I get paid? ______

How do I get paid? ______

______

Member # ______

STATUS: ❍ Active member ❍ Inactive member ❍ Cancelled

Contact Info ______

Username/Login ______

______

PIN or Code ______

Password/hint ______

______

Password/hint change ______

______

______

______

❑ ✔ if password/PIN are recorded in a separate location

NOTES ______

______

______

TYPE OF ONLINE ACCOUNT

❑ affiliate ❑ online store ❑ membership site ❑ digital storage
❑ service or software subscription ❑ other ______

Name of site/asset ______

Website address ______

______

❑ **This is a site I pay into**

How much do I pay? $ ______

How often do I pay? ______

How do I pay? ______

❑ **This is an income-generating site**

How often do I get paid? ______

How do I get paid? ______

______

Member # ______

STATUS: ❍ Active member ❍ Inactive member ❍ Cancelled

Contact Info ______

Username/Login ______

______

PIN or Code ______

Password/hint ______

______

Password/hint change ______

______

______

______

❑ ✔ if password/PIN are recorded in a separate location

NOTES

______

______

______

______

My digital life $ Affiliate, retail, etc.

TYPE OF ONLINE ACCOUNT

❑ affiliate ❑ online store ❑ membership site ❑ digital storage

❑ service or software subscription ❑ other ____________

Name of site/asset ____________

Website address ____________

____

❑ **This is a site I pay into**

How much do I pay? $ ____________

How often do I pay? ____________

How do I pay? ____________

❑ **This is an income-generating site**

How often do I get paid? ____________

How do I get paid? ____________

____

Member # ____________

STATUS: ❍ Active member ❍ Inactive member ❍ Cancelled

Contact Info ____________

Username/Login ____________

____

PIN or Code ____________

Password/hint ____________

____

Password/hint change ____________

____

____

____

❑ ✔ if password/PIN are recorded in a separate location

NOTES ____________

____

____

TYPE OF ONLINE ACCOUNT

❑ affiliate ❑ online store ❑ membership site ❑ digital storage

❑ service or software subscription ❑ other ______

Name of site/asset ______

Website address ______

______

❑ This is a site I pay into

How much do I pay? $ ______

How often do I pay? ______

How do I pay? ______

❑ This is an income-generating site

How often do I get paid? ______

How do I get paid? ______

______

Member # ______

STATUS: ❍ Active member ❍ Inactive member ❍ Cancelled

Contact Info ______

Username/Login ______

______

PIN or Code ______

Password/hint ______

______

Password/hint change ______

______

______

______

❑ ✔ if password/PIN are recorded in a separate location

NOTES

______

______

______

______

My digital life $ Affiliate, retail, etc.

TYPE OF ONLINE ACCOUNT

❑ affiliate ❑ online store ❑ membership site ❑ digital storage

❑ service or software subscription ❑ other ______________________

Name of site/asset ______________________

Website address ______________________

____

❑ **This is a site I pay into**

How much do I pay? $ ______________________

How often do I pay? ______________________

How do I pay? ______________________

❑ **This is an income-generating site**

How often do I get paid? ______________________

How do I get paid? ______________________

____

Member # ______________________

STATUS: ❍ Active member ❍ Inactive member ❍ Cancelled

Contact Info ______________________

Username/Login ______________________

____

PIN or Code ______________________

Password/hint ______________________

____

Password/hint change ______________________

____

____

____

❑ ✔ if password/PIN are recorded in a separate location

NOTES ______________________

____

____

TYPE OF ONLINE ACCOUNT

❑ affiliate ❑ online store ❑ membership site ❑ digital storage
❑ service or software subscription ❑ other ______________

Name of site/asset ______________

Website address ______________

____

❑ This is a site I pay into

How much do I pay? $ ______________

How often do I pay? ______________

How do I pay? ______________

❑ This is an income-generating site

How often do I get paid? ______________

How do I get paid? ______________

____

Member # ______________

STATUS: ❍ Active member ❍ Inactive member ❍ Cancelled

Contact Info ______________

Username/Login ______________

____

PIN or Code ______________

Password/hint ______________

____

Password/hint change ______________

____

____

____

❑ ✔ if password/PIN are recorded in a separate location

NOTES

____

____

____

____

My digital life $ Affiliate, retail, etc.

TYPE OF ONLINE ACCOUNT

❑ affiliate ❑ online store ❑ membership site ❑ digital storage

❑ service or software subscription ❑ other ____________

Name of site/asset ____________

Website address ____________

____

❑ **This is a site I pay into**

How much do I pay? $ ____________

How often do I pay? ____________

How do I pay? ____________

❑ **This is an income-generating site**

How often do I get paid? ____________

How do I get paid? ____________

____

Member # ____________

STATUS: ❍ Active member ❍ Inactive member ❍ Cancelled

Contact Info ____________

Username/Login ____________

____

PIN or Code ____________

Password/hint ____________

____

Password/hint change ____________

____

____

____

❑ ✔ if password/PIN are recorded in a separate location

NOTES ____________

____

____

TYPE OF ONLINE ACCOUNT

❑ affiliate ❑ online store ❑ membership site ❑ digital storage

❑ service or software subscription ❑ other ______________________

Name of site/asset ______________________

Website address ______________________

____

❑ This is a site I pay into

How much do I pay? $ ______________________

How often do I pay? ______________________

How do I pay? ______________________

❑ This is an income-generating site

How often do I get paid? ______________________

How do I get paid? ______________________

____

Member # ______________________

STATUS: ❍ Active member ❍ Inactive member ❍ Cancelled

Contact Info ______________________

Username/Login ______________________

____

PIN or Code ______________________

Password/hint ______________________

____

Password/hint change ______________________

____

____

____

❑ ✔ if password/PIN are recorded in a separate location

NOTES

____

____

____

____

My digital life $ Affiliate, retail, etc.

TYPE OF ONLINE ACCOUNT

❑ affiliate ❑ online store ❑ membership site ❑ digital storage

❑ service or software subscription ❑ other ______

Name of site/asset ______

Website address ______

______

❑ **This is a site I pay into**

How much do I pay? $ ______

How often do I pay? ______

How do I pay? ______

❑ **This is an income-generating site**

How often do I get paid? ______

How do I get paid? ______

______

Member # ______

STATUS: ❍ Active member ❍ Inactive member ❍ Cancelled

Contact Info ______

Username/Login ______

______

PIN or Code ______

Password/hint ______

______

Password/hint change ______

______

______

______

❑ ✔ if password/PIN are recorded in a separate location

NOTES ______

______

______

TYPE OF ONLINE ACCOUNT

❑ affiliate ❑ online store ❑ membership site ❑ digital storage

❑ service or software subscription ❑ other ______________________

Name of site/asset ______________________

Website address ______________________

____

❑ This is a site I pay into

How much do I pay? $ ______________________

How often do I pay? ______________________

How do I pay? ______________________

❑ This is an income-generating site

How often do I get paid? ______________________

How do I get paid? ______________________

____

Member # ______________________

STATUS: ❍ Active member ❍ Inactive member ❍ Cancelled

Contact Info ______________________

Username/Login ______________________

____

PIN or Code ______________________

Password/hint ______________________

____

Password/hint change ______________________

____

____

____

❑ ✔ if password/PIN are recorded in a separate location

NOTES

____

____

____

____

My digital life $ Affiliate, retail, etc.

TYPE OF ONLINE ACCOUNT

❑ affiliate ❑ online store ❑ membership site ❑ digital storage
❑ service or software subscription ❑ other ____________

Name of site/asset ____________

Website address ____________

____

❑ **This is a site I pay into**

How much do I pay? $ ____________

How often do I pay? ____________

How do I pay? ____________

❑ **This is an income-generating site**

How often do I get paid? ____________

How do I get paid? ____________

____

Member # ____________

STATUS: ❍ Active member ❍ Inactive member ❍ Cancelled

Contact Info ____________

Username/Login ____________

____

PIN or Code ____________

Password/hint ____________

____

Password/hint change ____________

____

____

____

❑ ✔ if password/PIN are recorded in a separate location

NOTES ____________

____

____

TYPE OF ONLINE ACCOUNT

❑ affiliate ❑ online store ❑ membership site ❑ digital storage

❑ service or software subscription ❑ other ______________________

Name of site/asset ______________________

Website address ______________________

____

❑ This is a site I pay into

How much do I pay? $ ______________________

How often do I pay? ______________________

How do I pay? ______________________

❑ This is an income-generating site

How often do I get paid? ______________________

How do I get paid? ______________________

____

Member # ______________________

STATUS: ❍ Active member ❍ Inactive member ❍ Cancelled

Contact Info ______________________

Username/Login ______________________

____

PIN or Code ______________________

Password/hint ______________________

____

Password/hint change ______________________

____

____

____

❑ ✔ if password/PIN are recorded in a separate location

NOTES

____

____

____

____

My digital life $ Affiliate, retail, etc.

TYPE OF ONLINE ACCOUNT

❑ affiliate ❑ online store ❑ membership site ❑ digital storage

❑ service or software subscription ❑ other __________

Name of site/asset __________

Website address __________

❑ This is a site I pay into

How much do I pay? $ __________

How often do I pay? __________

How do I pay? __________

❑ This is an income-generating site

How often do I get paid? __________

How do I get paid? __________

Member # __________

STATUS: ❍ Active member ❍ Inactive member ❍ Cancelled

Contact Info __________

Username/Login __________

PIN or Code __________

Password/hint __________

Password/hint change __________

❑ ✔ if password/PIN are recorded in a separate location

NOTES __________

TYPE OF ONLINE ACCOUNT

❑ affiliate ❑ online store ❑ membership site ❑ digital storage

❑ service or software subscription ❑ other ______________

Name of site/asset ______________

Website address ______________

____

❑ **This is a site I pay into**

How much do I pay? $ ______________

How often do I pay? ______________

How do I pay? ______________

❑ **This is an income-generating site**

How often do I get paid? ______________

How do I get paid? ______________

____

Member # ______________

STATUS: ❍ Active member ❍ Inactive member ❍ Cancelled

Contact Info ______________

Username/Login ______________

____

PIN or Code ______________

Password/hint ______________

____

Password/hint change ______________

____

____

____

❑ ✔ if password/PIN are recorded in a separate location

NOTES

____

____

____

____

My digital life $ Affiliate, retail, etc.

TYPE OF ONLINE ACCOUNT

❑ affiliate ❑ online store ❑ membership site ❑ digital storage

❑ service or software subscription ❑ other ______________________

Name of site/asset ______________________

Website address ______________________

____

❑ This is a site I pay into

How much do I pay? $ ______________________

How often do I pay? ______________________

How do I pay? ______________________

❑ This is an income-generating site

How often do I get paid? ______________________

How do I get paid? ______________________

____

Member # ______________________

STATUS: ❍ Active member ❍ Inactive member ❍ Cancelled

Contact Info ______________________

Username/Login ______________________

____

PIN or Code ______________________

Password/hint ______________________

____

Password/hint change ______________________

____

____

____

❑ ✔ if password/PIN are recorded in a separate location

NOTES ______________________

____

____

TYPE OF ONLINE ACCOUNT

❑ affiliate ❑ online store ❑ membership site ❑ digital storage

❑ service or software subscription ❑ other ______________________

Name of site/asset ______________________

Website address ______________________

____

❑ This is a site I pay into

How much do I pay? $ ______________________

How often do I pay? ______________________

How do I pay? ______________________

❑ This is an income-generating site

How often do I get paid? ______________________

How do I get paid? ______________________

____

Member # ______________________

STATUS: ❍ Active member ❍ Inactive member ❍ Cancelled

Contact Info ______________________

Username/Login ______________________

____

PIN or Code ______________________

Password/hint ______________________

____

Password/hint change ______________________

____

____

____

❑ ✔ if password/PIN are recorded in a separate location

NOTES

____

____

____

____

My digital life $ Affiliate, retail, etc.

TYPE OF ONLINE ACCOUNT

❑ affiliate ❑ online store ❑ membership site ❑ digital storage

❑ service or software subscription ❑ other ______

Name of site/asset ______

Website address ______

______

❑ **This is a site I pay into**

How much do I pay? $ ______

How often do I pay? ______

How do I pay? ______

❑ **This is an income-generating site**

How often do I get paid? ______

How do I get paid? ______

______

Member # ______

STATUS: ❍ Active member ❍ Inactive member ❍ Cancelled

Contact Info ______

Username/Login ______

______

PIN or Code ______

Password/hint ______

______

Password/hint change ______

______

______

______

❑ ✔ if password/PIN are recorded in a separate location

NOTES ______

______

______

TYPE OF ONLINE ACCOUNT

❑ affiliate ❑ online store ❑ membership site ❑ digital storage

❑ service or software subscription ❑ other ______________________

Name of site/asset ______________________

Website address ______________________

____

❑ This is a site I pay into

How much do I pay? $ ______________________

How often do I pay? ______________________

How do I pay? ______________________

❑ This is an income-generating site

How often do I get paid? ______________________

How do I get paid? ______________________

____

Member # ______________________

STATUS: ❍ Active member ❍ Inactive member ❍ Cancelled

Contact Info ______________________

Username/Login ______________________

____

PIN or Code ______________________

Password/hint ______________________

____

Password/hint change ______________________

____

____

____

❑ ✔ if password/PIN are recorded in a separate location

NOTES

____

____

____

____

My digital life $ Affiliate, retail, etc.

TYPE OF ONLINE ACCOUNT

❑ affiliate ❑ online store ❑ membership site ❑ digital storage

❑ service or software subscription ❑ other ____________________

Name of site/asset ____________________

Website address ____________________

____

❑ This is a site I pay into

How much do I pay? $ ____________________

How often do I pay? ____________________

How do I pay? ____________________

❑ This is an income-generating site

How often do I get paid? ____________________

How do I get paid? ____________________

____

Member # ____________________

STATUS: ❍ Active member ❍ Inactive member ❍ Cancelled

Contact Info ____________________

Username/Login ____________________

____

PIN or Code ____________________

Password/hint ____________________

____

Password/hint change ____________________

____

____

____

❑ ✔ if password/PIN are recorded in a separate location

NOTES ____________________

____

____

TYPE OF ONLINE ACCOUNT

❑ affiliate ❑ online store ❑ membership site ❑ digital storage

❑ service or software subscription ❑ other ____________

Name of site/asset ____________

Website address ____________

____

❑ This is a site I pay into

How much do I pay? $ ____________

How often do I pay? ____________

How do I pay? ____________

❑ This is an income-generating site

How often do I get paid? ____________

How do I get paid? ____________

____

Member # ____________

STATUS: ❍ Active member ❍ Inactive member ❍ Cancelled

Contact Info ____________

Username/Login ____________

____

PIN or Code ____________

Password/hint ____________

____

Password/hint change ____________

____

____

____

❑ ✔ if password/PIN are recorded in a separate location

NOTES

____

____

____

____

My digital life $ Affiliate, retail, etc.

TYPE OF ONLINE ACCOUNT

❑ affiliate ❑ online store ❑ membership site ❑ digital storage

❑ service or software subscription ❑ other ______

Name of site/asset ______

Website address ______

______

❑ **This is a site I pay into**

How much do I pay? $ ______

How often do I pay? ______

How do I pay? ______

❑ **This is an income-generating site**

How often do I get paid? ______

How do I get paid? ______

______

Member # ______

STATUS: ❍ Active member ❍ Inactive member ❍ Cancelled

Contact Info ______

Username/Login ______

______

PIN or Code ______

Password/hint ______

______

Password/hint change ______

______

______

______

❑ ✔ if password/PIN are recorded in a separate location

NOTES ______

______

______

TYPE OF ONLINE ACCOUNT

❑ affiliate ❑ online store ❑ membership site ❑ digital storage

❑ service or software subscription ❑ other ____________________

Name of site/asset ____________________

Website address ____________________

____

❑ This is a site I pay into

How much do I pay? $ ____________________

How often do I pay? ____________________

How do I pay? ____________________

❑ This is an income-generating site

How often do I get paid? ____________________

How do I get paid? ____________________

____

Member # ____________________

STATUS: ❍ Active member ❍ Inactive member ❍ Cancelled

Contact Info ____________________

Username/Login ____________________

____

PIN or Code ____________________

Password/hint ____________________

____

Password/hint change ____________________

____

____

____

❑ ✔ if password/PIN are recorded in a separate location

NOTES

____

____

____

____

My digital life $ Affiliate, retail, etc.

TYPE OF ONLINE ACCOUNT

❑ affiliate ❑ online store ❑ membership site ❑ digital storage
❑ service or software subscription ❑ other ______

Name of site/asset ______

Website address ______

______

❑ **This is a site I pay into**

How much do I pay? $ ______

How often do I pay? ______

How do I pay? ______

❑ **This is an income-generating site**

How often do I get paid? ______

How do I get paid? ______

______

Member # ______

STATUS: ❍ Active member ❍ Inactive member ❍ Cancelled

Contact Info ______

Username/Login ______

______

PIN or Code ______

Password/hint ______

______

Password/hint change ______

______

______

______

❑ ✔ if password/PIN are recorded in a separate location

NOTES ______

______

______

TYPE OF ONLINE ACCOUNT

❑ affiliate ❑ online store ❑ membership site ❑ digital storage

❑ service or software subscription ❑ other ______

Name of site/asset ______

Website address ______

❑ **This is a site I pay into**

How much do I pay? $ ______

How often do I pay? ______

How do I pay? ______

❑ **This is an income-generating site**

How often do I get paid? ______

How do I get paid? ______

Member # ______

STATUS: ❍ Active member ❍ Inactive member ❍ Cancelled

Contact Info ______

Username/Login ______

PIN or Code ______

Password/hint ______

Password/hint change ______

❑ ✔ if password/PIN are recorded in a separate location

NOTES

My digital life $ Affiliate, retail, etc.

TYPE OF ONLINE ACCOUNT

❑ affiliate ❑ online store ❑ membership site ❑ digital storage

❑ service or software subscription ❑ other ______________________

Name of site/asset ______________________

Website address ______________________

____

❑ **This is a site I pay into**

How much do I pay? $ ______________________

How often do I pay? ______________________

How do I pay? ______________________

❑ **This is an income-generating site**

How often do I get paid? ______________________

How do I get paid? ______________________

____

Member # ______________________

STATUS: ❍ Active member ❍ Inactive member ❍ Cancelled

Contact Info ______________________

Username/Login ______________________

____

PIN or Code ______________________

Password/hint ______________________

____

Password/hint change ______________________

____

____

____

❑ ✔ if password/PIN are recorded in a separate location

NOTES ______________________

____

____

TYPE OF ONLINE ACCOUNT

❑ affiliate ❑ online store ❑ membership site ❑ digital storage

❑ service or software subscription ❑ other ______________________

Name of site/asset ______________________

Website address ______________________

____

❑ This is a site I pay into

How much do I pay? $ ______________________

How often do I pay? ______________________

How do I pay? ______________________

❑ This is an income-generating site

How often do I get paid? ______________________

How do I get paid? ______________________

____

Member # ______________________

STATUS: ❍ Active member ❍ Inactive member ❍ Cancelled

Contact Info ______________________

Username/Login ______________________

____

PIN or Code ______________________

Password/hint ______________________

____

Password/hint change ______________________

____

____

____

❑ ✔ if password/PIN are recorded in a separate location

NOTES

____

____

____

____

Let Family Know™

Email Accounts

Let Family Know®

EMAIL ACCOUNT

Email address

____

____

❑ Personal ❑ Business ❑ Other ________________

____

Phone number associated with the account ________________

Postal code associated with the account ________________

Backup email ________________

Username/login ________________

Password/hint ________________

____

Password/hint change ________________

____

____

____

____

____

____

____

____

____

NOTE ________________

____

____

❑ ✔ if password is recorded in a separate location

EMAIL ACCOUNT

Email address ______

______

❑ Personal ❑ Business ❑ Other ______

______

Phone number associated with the account ______

Postal code associated with the account ______

Backup email ______

Username/login ______

Password/hint ______

______

Password/hint change ______

______

______

______

______

______

______

______

______

______

NOTE ______

______

______

❑ ✔ if password is recorded in a separate location

My digital life

Email

EMAIL ACCOUNT

Email address

❑ Personal ❑ Business ❑ Other

Phone number associated with the account

Postal code associated with the account

Backup email

Username/login

Password/hint

Password/hint change

NOTE

❑ ✔ if password is recorded in a separate location

EMAIL ACCOUNT

Email address

❑ Personal ❑ Business ❑ Other

Phone number associated with the account

Postal code associated with the account

Backup email

Username/login

Password/hint

Password/hint change

NOTE

❑ ✔ if password is recorded in a separate location

My digital life

Email

EMAIL ACCOUNT

Email address

❑ Personal ❑ Business ❑ Other

Phone number associated with the account

Postal code associated with the account

Backup email

Username/login

Password/hint

Password/hint change

NOTE

❑ ✔ if password is recorded in a separate location

EMAIL ACCOUNT

Email address

____

____

❑ Personal ❑ Business ❑ Other ______________________________

____

Phone number associated with the account ______________________________

Postal code associated with the account ______________________________

Backup email ______________________________

Username/login ______________________________

Password/hint ______________________________

____

Password/hint change ______________________________

____

____

____

____

____

____

____

____

____

NOTE ______________________________

____

____

❑ ✔ if password is recorded in a separate location

EMAIL ACCOUNT

Email address

❑ Personal ❑ Business ❑ Other

Phone number associated with the account

Postal code associated with the account

Backup email

Username/login

Password/hint

Password/hint change

NOTE

❑ ✔ if password is recorded in a separate location

EMAIL ACCOUNT

Email address

____

____

❑ Personal ❑ Business ❑ Other ______________________________

____

Phone number associated with the account ______________________________

Postal code associated with the account ______________________________

Backup email ______________________________

Username/login ______________________________

Password/hint ______________________________

____

Password/hint change ______________________________

____

____

____

____

____

____

____

____

____

NOTE ______________________________

____

____

❑ ✔ if password is recorded in a separate location

EMAIL ACCOUNT

Email address

____

____

❑ Personal ❑ Business ❑ Other ______________________

____

Phone number associated with the account ______________________

Postal code associated with the account ______________________

Backup email ______________________

Username/login ______________________

Password/hint ______________________

____

Password/hint change ______________________

____

____

____

____

____

____

____

____

____

NOTE ______________________

____

____

❑ ✔ if password is recorded in a separate location

EMAIL ACCOUNT

Email address

____

____

❑ Personal ❑ Business ❑ Other ____________________

____

Phone number associated with the account ____________________

Postal code associated with the account ____________________

Backup email ____________________

Username/login ____________________

Password/hint ____________________

____

Password/hint change ____________________

____

____

____

____

____

____

____

____

____

NOTE ____________________

____

____

❑ ✔ if password is recorded in a separate location

My digital life

Email

EMAIL ACCOUNT

Email address

❑ Personal ❑ Business ❑ Other

Phone number associated
with the account

Postal code associated
with the account

Backup email

Username/login

Password/hint

Password/hint change

NOTE

❑ ✔ if password is recorded in a separate location

EMAIL ACCOUNT

Email address

❑ Personal ❑ Business ❑ Other

Phone number associated with the account

Postal code associated with the account

Backup email

Username/login

Password/hint

Password/hint change

NOTE

❑ ✔ if password is recorded in a separate location

EMAIL ACCOUNT

Email address

____

____

❑ Personal ❑ Business ❑ Other ______________________________

____

Phone number associated with the account ______________________________

Postal code associated with the account ______________________________

Backup email ______________________________

Username/login ______________________________

Password/hint ______________________________

____

Password/hint change ______________________________

____

____

____

____

____

____

____

____

____

NOTE ______________________________

____

____

❑ ✔ if password is recorded in a separate location

EMAIL ACCOUNT

Email address

____

____

❑ Personal ❑ Business ❑ Other ______________

____

Phone number associated
with the account ______________________________

Postal code associated
with the account ______________________________

Backup email ______________________________

Username/login ______________________________

Password/hint ______________________________

____

Password/hint change ______________________________

____

____

____

____

____

____

____

____

____

NOTE ______________________________

____

____

❑ ✔ if password is recorded in a separate location

EMAIL ACCOUNT

Email address

❑ Personal ❑ Business ❑ Other

Phone number associated with the account

Postal code associated with the account

Backup email

Username/login

Password/hint

Password/hint change

NOTE

❑ ✔ if password is recorded in a separate location

EMAIL ACCOUNT

Email address

____

____

❑ Personal ❑ Business ❑ Other ____________________

____

Phone number associated with the account ____________________

Postal code associated with the account ____________________

Backup email ____________________

Username/login ____________________

Password/hint ____________________

____

Password/hint change ____________________

____

____

____

____

____

____

____

____

____

NOTE ____________________

____

____

❑ ✔ if password is recorded in a separate location

My digital life

Email

EMAIL ACCOUNT

Email address

____

____

❑ Personal ❑ Business ❑ Other ____________________

____

Phone number associated
with the account ____________________

Postal code associated
with the account ____________________

Backup email ____________________

Username/login ____________________

Password/hint ____________________

____

Password/hint change ____________________

____

____

____

____

____

____

____

____

____

NOTE ____________________

____

____

❑ ✔ if password is recorded in a separate location

EMAIL ACCOUNT

Email address

❑ Personal ❑ Business ❑ Other

Phone number associated with the account

Postal code associated with the account

Backup email

Username/login

Password/hint

Password/hint change

NOTE

❑ ✔ if password is recorded in a separate location

My digital life

Email

EMAIL ACCOUNT

Email address

❑ Personal ❑ Business ❑ Other

Phone number associated with the account

Postal code associated with the account

Backup email

Username/login

Password/hint

Password/hint change

NOTE

❑ ✔ if password is recorded in a separate location

EMAIL ACCOUNT

Email address

❑ Personal ❑ Business ❑ Other

Phone number associated with the account

Postal code associated with the account

Backup email

Username/login

Password/hint

Password/hint change

NOTE

❑ ✔ if password is recorded in a separate location

Let Family Know®

Helping you organize information that matters

Protecting Personal and Financial Information in the Internet Age

even if you say you are "barely online."

Lots of great tips you'll want to share

Let Family Know®

Introduction

In the wake of massive data breaches at websites as significant as Equifax, the idea of total security is starting to feel like a myth. And yet, you can keep your personal information safe and secure, if you take the necessary steps to do so.

While it is true that there are always unrecognized "back doors" into even the most secure networks, websites and devices, you can stay a bit farther ahead of the curve than most average consumers, and even many businesses.

How?

That's what we are going to explore in these few information-dense pages, about optimal security for your financial accounts and other relevant, personal data.

It is about more than just keeping passwords safe, and it is also a lot more than just keeping your data under wraps. It is about protecting your identity, credit and even your physical property safe and secure.

A short story

Let's begin with a short and cautionary tale about what can happen to a modern consumer who fails to protect their information.

We'll call this person "Sam". He got an odd email from a friend, and fellow musician, telling him that the download he'd asked about was attached. It looked like the friend's email, so Sam clicked on it. He had to enter his email password to open the file, and then nothing happened.

He called the friend and asked what that was about, but the friend said he'd never sent anything. Within a few hours, Sam couldn't get into his email account, social media and got an alert from the bank that someone was trying to change the login credentials for his online banking, and was it him?

In moments, your unprotected information can be stolen. Even worse for Sam was that he had been emailing himself his updated passwords to other accounts, and now that hacker had it all – logins to everything.

Like Sam, many of us don't quite know how to best manage our online security, passwords and login credentials. We type them up and print them out to hang on a nearby bulletin board in the office. We might just jot them down in a pad next to the computer. We may just use a simple word like "Password" to log into things on our phones.

Disaster awaits all who use these methods.

The good news is that you can easily protect yourself and your login credentials with simple steps.

In the pages that follow, we are going to learn about potential pitfalls and how to avoid and/or overcome them to keep yourself and your data as safe as possible in the age of "online everything".

What needs protecting?

It goes by many different names:

- Secure information
- Personal data/information
- Internet identity
- Sensitive information
- Financial data, and more
-

In fact, one expert says that a key to online security is **deciding what PII or Personally Identifiable Information is to you**. He explains it like this:

"The traditional definition of personally identifying information (PII) -- health records, credit card numbers, social security number, etc. -- is so 20th century. The big data age of the Internet is upon us, and even data not previously considered to be PII can feel very personal when viewed in a broader context... [and] may include such information as your email address, browsing history and search history... [and] is going to be broadened as we move further into the information society."

Let's not forget things like government issued ID numbers, account numbers, school and work logins, and so much more.

The bottom line is that it is all about YOU.

It's your information and it's the data that serves as the foundation of your everyday life. If you don't believe it, just consider that one person with a single email address is also likely to have identities at their bank(s), social media sites, and dozens of accounts at other sites that can range as wide as their utility company or credit card companies to their shopping cart login for their favorite sites.

And in that rather narrow assortment of sites, your social security number, full name, address, phone numbers, email address and even security information such as your mother's maiden name, work or residential history and current location might be easily identified. Your surfing and browsing activities are in there, too, and even this may compromise your information and security.

In other words, even if you say you are "barely online", you are still vulnerable to threats to your identity, financial and credit information, and all other data; and that means that the answer posed by the title of this section is simple.

***"What needs protecting?"* Everything.**

But this becomes even more significant when we realize that there are just a few ways that all of that information is protected. Usually, it involves nothing more than a registered account, username and password. With just a few steps, a dedicated thief and hacker could gain entry into all of your data.

So, how do you protect *everything*? Let's find out ...

Start with the devices

If we are going to be sure that all of your personal and secure information is as protected as possible, we have to start with where it's found.

In other words, where does your data live?

For most, it's on a desktop or laptop, but also on a tablet or two as well as our mobile phones and offline storage devices like USB drives, SIM cards and free standing hard drives. That means your first step is to be sure that you **secure all of your devices**.

Doing that is not as simple as PIN or password protecting them or ensuring they are physically secure (including being aware of "shoulder surfers" watching your every move and leaving unlocked devices unattended).

It also means ensuring you have:

- **Up to date anti-virus software in place**
- **Anti-malware and anti-ransomware software** active on the system
- **A firewall installed and running**
- **All the operating system (OS) security** patches and updates installed
- **Secure web browsers**, and ensure that they are always up to date
- **Apps that are up to date** and from authenticated sources
- **Apps that are configured with the utmost privacy** – the MyPermissions.com site is a very handy tool for setting all apps to the most private and secure
- **Prevented apps and software from updating automatically** without first prompting you to review and approve the changes, with the exception of the OS.Set devices to lock after a brief period of inactivity
- **Activated any "wipe your phone/device" features available**. Why? If your device is stolen and without any chance at recovery, the wipe feature eliminates any threats that the information on the phone creates.

- **Started to be MORE than just wary of public Wi-Fi** as it is one of the easiest ways to have data, identity, money and control of a device stolen.
- **Destroyed hardware before disposing of it.** You can get a tremendous amount of data out of old machines, and the only way to protect yourself is to make sure that the old hard drives are entirely unreadable before you dispose of them. Sanitizing is done by shredding the original disk drive, magnetically erasing the disk or using modern software to wipe it.
- **Powered down.** Want to protect your data the easiest way possible? Never leave a computer running unless it is in use!
- **Logged out of admin.** The technology experts of the world warn that your computer use should be done at the PoLP level. This is the Principle of Least Privilege level without any admin rights. Surfing as an admin leaves the system vulnerable to all exploits, but if your computer does not see you as a user with any admin-level rights, many attacks are ended before they begin.
- **Disabled Bluetooth** if you are not using it as this is a common "back door" for identity thieves and hackers
- **Explore sandboxing.** This is an emerging form of security but very handy as it works against "drive by downloads" full of malicious code. It allows a browser to only use the resources needed to do its work, and "any other piece of software that tries to install itself, such as a virus, will be blocked. At the time of this writing, only one browser includes sandboxing by default: Google Chrome." You can use Sandboxie on Windows computers to protect yourself when using other browsers.

"Phew!"

I hear you, that is a lot, but that is only the beginning. Physically securing and updating your devices is just a solid first step. Stop reading now and begin doing all of those steps just outlined.

Then, you need to factor in the networks and more.

Consider VPNs at home and in public

Security, where devices are concerned, might also mean **using a VPN** to surf at home or in public as a way to totally lock down your security.

The VPN or Virtual Private Network is a way of encrypting information and reducing such issues as tracking, hacking and more. They are not available for free, and there are hundreds at the time this was written, but they are a great way to protect your privacy and your data.

As the famous Gizmodo website has said:

> *"...the Internet is still a digital jungle where hackers easily steal sensitive information from the ill-equipped ... VPNs, or Virtual Private Networks, allow users to securely access a private network and share data remotely through public networks. Much like a firewall protects your data on your computer, VPNs protect it online... Because VPNs use a combination of dedicated connections and encryption protocols to generate virtual P2P connections, even if snoopers did manage to siphon off some of the transmitted data, they'd be unable to access it on account of the encryption."*

Take a few moments to run an Internet search for VPNs. You'll see scores of them. Shop around and find one in your budget and that rates highly. Then, use it!

GPS or not?

You might also have to **reconsider the use of GPS**. While the built in GPS in most mobile devices is great when using it to navigate, looking for a lost device or letting yourself be geographically tracked for social "check ins", it can also compromise your data (and personal) security.

With that in mind, think about GPS as something to enable – **use only when needed** and don't allow all apps to track you. Understand that anything you share in terms of GPS can often be shared between sites, i.e. Twitter and Facebook sharing. Also remember that all of your photos may be geotagged with location data, which can tell people precisely where you are, leaving your devices open to security threats, and in many instances, your home, too.

Yet, even with all of this security, you have to remember that your devices all connect to a network (via a home router, Wi-Fi hotspot or through your mobile provider). That means that true security is not limited to simply making your devices difficult to access, but also ***paying attention to the use of networks and the Internet in general***.

In other words, your security starts with the devices you use, but goes far beyond that alone. It is why we said a VPN is a good idea, but there's more to the story.

Confused already?

Most people are somewhat overwhelmed by the idea of keeping things safe, and say *"Fine, if it's THAT difficult, I'll just write things down!"*

So, they then use pencil and paper documents to record user names and passwords. Yet, even that is not totally foolproof either, because data can still be compromised by breaches on the websites used, and by the individual themselves if they don't understand things like Spam, phishing and weak passwords.

The basic rundown

So, let's first do a brief list of everything that needs to be addressed, and then we'll look at simple tips for tackling the more complex issues.

- **The Devices.** We've already looked into this issue, so use the criteria suggested above – installing all of the safeguards available and instituting better physical security policies if needed.
- **Going paperless.** This may seem unrelated to online security, but if you eliminate one major threat – paper documents that can be stolen or used to obtain account or personal data – you eliminate a big portion of the trouble.

Just consider this simple example:

Sara was determined to be totally secure. She used one credit card, registered only one bank account online, and limited her use of the Internet to email alone.

She opened her credit card statement one day to see that she had several hundred dollars of unauthorized (i.e. fraudulent) charges at an electronics store three states away. In the end, she discovered that her paper credit card statement had been opened, the data stolen, and the purchases made almost an entire month before she realized it. If she was paperless, not only would the paperwork have been unavailable to a thief, but she would have seen the purchases appear in her online activity (and been able to create account alerts) weeks earlier.

So, staying offline is no guarantee, and whenever you can go paperless, you should do so. And if you prefer not to? Shred everything before tossing it out, and make a point of checking your accounts online in between printed statements. Consider account usage alerts that you receive via text when a purchase is made, and other similar protections, too.

Also, know precisely what to do if you are a victim of identity theft (online or the real world), starting with the Federal Trade Commission's advice and support.
https://www.consumer.ftc.gov/features/feature-0014-identity-theft

- **Make killer passwords.** Don't worry – we are going to consider the many ways to use "impossible to crack" passwords and optimal password management policies in a moment. The point here is to understand that they are a major part of security.
- **Be smart with email.** There are some amazingly convincing tactics that scammers use to trick you into turning over data or even the control of your online identities. Email is one of their favorite approaches, so we'll need to take a close look at it, too.
- **Think about social media.** Facebook may be fun, but it is not the best place for protecting privacy and keeping your data secure. We'll spend a few minutes looking at the ways you are compromised...and you may find it better to just delete social media from your life!
- **Backup data.** This creates duplicates in the event of loss, and the best place to backup is not a piece of paper tacked to the wall. Instead, it is the cloud. It places all of your information in a place accessible only to yourself and has nothing to do with a local device. It is a wonderful form of "disaster recovery" as well as an impenetrable form of security, *but only if it is encrypted and password protected*. You can also use secure and encrypted offline devices instead – think USB drives and Security Information Management Systems (SIMs).

- **Store information offline.** While we've said that writing it down or creating a spreadsheet to track your usernames and passwords is common enough, that is not the kind of "secure offline storage" we mean or even advise.

  Instead, simply put information on offline devices (SIM cards and USB drives are the most common) that are fully encrypted. If it is stolen or lost, no one can use the sensitive data contained. And for goodness sake, never (read that as NEVER) store passwords with the device (a note with login details or a paper tacked to the wall near the laptop) are the same as leaving your keys in your car's ignition.

- **Secure the network.** Whether it is in your home or your office, you need the network to be locked and password protected at the very least. It is best if your networks are actually secured with passwords, encrypted, and hidden. This prevents them from showing up whenever someone is looking for nearby Wi-Fi networks. And if you use a VPN, it makes security a certainty.

- **Be smart online.** Use only secure websites when shopping, install the HTTPS Everywhere extension to encrypt everything, never download anything from unknown sites, opt out of ad tracking, and try to *avoid using your browser's password saving* as it can leave you wide open to trouble if your system is hacked.

These are the fundamentals for protecting your identity and your credit online. Now, let's delve a bit deeper into some of them as they are the most important elements in security.

✔ Passwords

There are passwords and then there are secure passwords.

The Identity Theft Resource Center says that a strong password must have eight characters or more and feature lower and upper case letters, at least one digit and at least one special character.

They are also best when free of easily guessed words, numeric combinations, and other details easily gleaned from online profiles such as your Facebook page or a Google search. They should never use your personally identifiable information (PII) – especially the social security number.

"We'll never guess her password."

You should also avoid using the same password for more than a single account or service. Why? Once one is cracked, it makes it amazingly easy for a hacker to take over almost an entire identity.

And never ever re-use the password to your main email account. As one expert warned, the hacker who has that also *"has the keys to your [virtual] kingdom. Passwords from the other sites you visit can be reset via your main email account. A criminal can trawl through your emails and find a treasure trove of personal data: from banking to passport details, including your date of birth, all of which enables ID fraud."*

This is also why you should have a secondary email account as it lets you have one that is dedicated to the more vulnerable data such as your financial and personal data, and the other can be used for shopping sites, social media and the rest. One can also be used to recover the other, which is great if you are hacked or forget login details.

You should also implement two-step verification whenever you login from a new or previously unused device. This blends the security of your email with whatever site you are attempting to access.

Indiana University suggested the use of "passphrases" rather than passwords. This is a *"different way of thinking about a much longer password. Dictionary words and names are no longer restricted. In fact, one of the very few restrictions is the length – 15 characters. Your passphrase can be a favorite song lyric, quote from a book, magazine, or movie, or something your kids said last week."* They also said that you might think of a *"saying or series of words that is easy for you to remember, and use the first letter of each word in the phrase, along with a combination of numbers and special characters, as your passphrase."*

So, how on earth do you memorize a handful of usernames and passwords? One answer is to use password management software. It's a way to store everything—but it is still requires YOU to be responsible. It's up to YOU to update the information or use an option that asks you if changes should be stored (when noticed). There are many applications available for different OS and devices – use one you trust and that is proven safe and effective. As of this writing, a few that rank high in an online search include RoboForm, 1password and Dashlane – and there are more. Just choose the one that fits your needs and budget and use it for all devices!

A great way to choose and organize passwords is also by "groupings". For example, create a specific type of password for your financial institutions but an entirely different type for social media. This can make it easier to memorize them, but also stops a hacker from gaining full access to your entire life if they break one set.

Never share your password, even with family members as they may have bad habits that include writing things down or inputting the information into a mobile device.

You might be doing this – but it's advised not to – is writing down your passwords, whether in a notebook, a spreadsheet or a sticky note. >> Instead, consider writing down a ***password hint*** or ***clue*** that lets you recall the terms or phrases chosen.

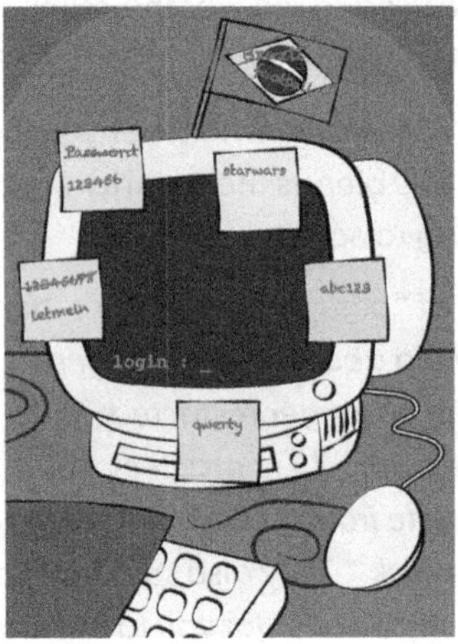

Many of us are too relaxed about this #1 rule: Don't leave passwords where anyone else can see them.

And even better is to think about storing sensitive data "locally".

You can use an encrypted and secure cloud provider to store all of your login credentials and information, but you may be even better protected by keeping everything offline.

As advised earlier, "consider backing up your most sensitive information locally or on a removable storage device you can keep under tight wraps... keep only those files which you need to access frequently and avoid putting up documents containing passwords for your various online accounts or personally identifiable information (PII) such as your credit card numbers, national identification number, home address, etc. If you must include these information in your files, make sure to encrypt them before you upload."

✔ Email

Email is a serious liability but something we all use and require. That means you need to understand how your information is vulnerable here. Generally, it is through Spam, phishing and malware that is activated when you open and interact with a fraudulent email messages, attachments or websites to which you sent via an embedded URL.

That means your standard approach to email should be:

- **Never click on a link you did not expect** – even if it seems like it is coming from a valid site. If you get an email telling you to log in through a link embedded in the email – DON'T. Instead, go to the site itself, login like usual and see if there is any sort of communication. Phone the company, but never open an unexpected message and link.
- **Skip emails from unknown parties**, and delete them immediately if you see there are also attachments.
- **Never share your secure email address** with anyone or any site you don't know
- **Avoid sending any sensitive information** via an unencrypted email
- **Learn how to identify phishing**, which is when cybercriminals seek information using malicious software hidden in an email message or even a website. Some major clues are generic greetings from someone who supposedly knows you, urgency in the overall tone of the message, spelling errors, weird links and odd requests for action.
- **Continually add Spam messages to your Spam folder** to help your email provider recognize the good from the bad.
- **Unsubscribe from unwanted messages**

You also want to block anyone who is communicating with you via email using options like social media. And you then want to head to the social media site to block them there, too.

✔ Social Media Safety

Though you might wonder where there are connections between things like your credit cards and banking accounts and your Facebook or other social media data, there is no real mystery.

Consider this simple illustration: Your social media page shows your holiday photos in real time. In other words, you are saying "Hey, we're not home!" Now, that alone is a problem. However, if someone can see information like your address, birthday, family relationships, and all other information, it makes it easier than ever for them to steal your identity.

Let's say you are a fan of a certain team and you talk about them a lot on your timeline. We see you are also a graduate of the college to which that team belongs AND you boast about the year you graduated. It is not a stretch for someone to guess that one or more passwords might have to do with the team, school or graduation date.

They can also see your hometown, your parents' names, your children's' names and birthdates...see the possibilities here?

That is just from a single social media account. When you have Facebook, Twitter, Instagram, LinkedIn, Pinterest and the rest, it is a treasure trove for the would-be thieves. It is also extremely useful to those who already have data, such as information purchased from the "dark web" as a result of one of the many, all-too-often, data breaches.

Give away nothing by making profiles private with the exception of "friends" and no one else. Remove all personal data. Never announce your current whereabouts and even stop sites from tracking.

The Ghostery extension for the Chrome browser, for example, blocks and assesses the different trackers found on any web page you use. There is also the Disconnect for Facebook extension that just stops Facebook from tracking. Using such options can really enhance your online security and the privacy you need for optimal safety.

In the end, many people concerned with privacy are actually just deleting their accounts at many social media sites; until those sites can ensure far better protections and guarantees of privacy.

In the event of disaster

What do you do if you discover a breach or some sort of threat to your security, here is some basic step by step advice:

- **Know the warning signs of a data breach** such as strange emails, unapproved purchases, inquiries or requests for your credit report, and so on
- **Verify that a breach has compromised your data** – Sites like Have I Been Pwned? are quite handy if you suspect someone has hacked or stolen data. (https://haveibeenpwned.com)
- **Take back control of your email accounts immediately** as this is a powerful tool in the hands of a hacker. They can request and reset login information for almost everything from here, so you MUST maintain control of it
- **If you see you are compromised** by using a website to check or because of problems with your identity, credit and so on – immediately change all of your passwords on every single account. Start with financial and work your way down, skipping none.
- **Contact your financial providers** and ask for new credit/debit cards.
- **Consider doing a credit freeze** with the three main credit agencies as this prevents a thief from getting your credit report
- **Institute credit monitoring** – use the free services or go the whole way and pay for non-stop monitoring at all levels
- **Alert friends and family** to the fact and ask them to tell you if they've gotten strange emails, social media messages and so on

Conclusion

We'll say it again – PHEW! That is a lot, but you've got to remember that hackers, scammers and thieves stop at nothing to get our valuable information. Your passwords and usernames are really the keys to it all.

In this short guide, we've reviewed what you can do to protect your passwords, whether you use the offline approach or you rely on a reputable password manager. You've learned other steps to protecting yourself, and hopefully you won't end up like Sam or others who find themselves seriously compromised and struggling to regain their identity, control their credit and even recover serious financial losses.

Start with your devices and networks, use killer password protocols, be wary with email and social media and you should be good to go – online and everywhere else!

Sources

https://digitalguardian.com/blog/101-data-protection-tips-how-keep-your-passwords-financial-personal-information-safe

https://gizmodo.com/5990192/vpns-what-they-do-how-they-work-and-why-youre-dumb-for-not-using-one

https://www.consumer.ftc.gov/features/feature-0014-identity-theft

https://www.theguardian.com/technology/2013/may/12/20-ways-keep-internet-identity-safe

https://www.consumer.ftc.gov/articles/0003-phishing

IMPORTANT ... PLEASE READ

TERMS OF USE

The Let Family Know® books, journals, planners, and organizers are sold with the understanding that the publisher is not engaged in providing legal, accounting or other professional service. Use of the products and websites produced by Let Family Know® LLC do not constitute legal advice—but rather, they are tools designed to simplify and make easier, the creation of information you would want people to know if anything should happen that would end your life or render you unable to communicate or make decisions. The journals, planners and organizers offer simple, fill-in-the-blank forms and pages that are not prepared nor customized by Let Family Know to meet any one person's particular needs.

We are not licensed to practice law, nor do we imply that these tools can substitute for legal advice. Where legal matters are concerned, we urge you to seek advice from a professional attorney who is licensed to practice law in the state in which you reside. Or, when looking for expert assistance on protecting your estate, your heirs or finances, consult with an estate attorney or professional estate planner who knows the laws in your state (as every state has different laws governing wills and estates), and who can help you design a plan to achieve the outcome you desire.

Let Family Know® tools, information and products are not intended to create or imply any attorney-client relationship.

NO WARRANTY. THIS JOURNAL AND ITS FORMS ARE PROVIDED ON AN "AS IS" BASIS. TO THE FULLEST EXTENT PERMITTED BY LAW, Let Family Know® LLC expressly disclaims any warranty of any kind, whether express or implied,about the warranty of merchantability, fitness for a particular purpose, title and non-infringement.

Let Family Know® LLC makes no warranty that (A) the books, journals, planners, organizers or information will meet your requirements; (B) that the results that may be obtained from the use of the materials will be accurate or reliable; or (C) the quality of the products or information, or other material or services purchased from the company by you will meet your expectations.

Obtaining this Journal or any materials from Let Family Know LLC, is done at your own discretion and at your own risk. Let Family Know LLC, and its publishers, shall have no responsibility.

Continued ...

LIMITATION OF LIABILITY AND INDEMNIFICATION

You will hold Let Family Know LLC and its officers, directors, employees and agents harmless for any indirect, punitive, special, incidental, or consequential damage, however it arises (including attorney's fees and all related costs and expenses of litigation and arbitration or arbitration instituted), whether in an action of contract, negligence, or other tortuous action, or arising out of or in connection with this agreement, including without limitation any claim for personal injury or property damage, arising form this agreement, and any violation by me of any Federal, State or Local laws, statutes, rules or regulations, even if Let Family Know had been previously advised of the possibility of such damage. If there is liability found on the part of Let Family Know LLC, it will be limited to the amount paid for the products and/or services and under no circumstances will there be consequential or punitive damages. Some states do not allow the exclusion or limitation of incidental or consequential damages, so the above limitation or exclusion may not apply to me. Further, except as permitted by law, nothing in this paragraph is intended to modify the provisions of California business and Professions Code Sections 6400, ET SEQ.

ACKNOWLEDGEMENT

*** By using Let Family Know® products or services, you acknowledge you have read these terms of use and agree to be bound by them.

www.LetFamilyKnow.com

More titles from Let Family Know®

8.5″ x 11″ books with planning worksheets or forms

How to Keep Family Stories, Traditions, and Values from Fading: *Recall and record years of your life ... in just minutes each week.*

How to Decide Who Will Inherit Your Stuff: *7 basic estate-planning steps that turn procrastination into peace of mind.*

Dear ___________, *A guide to writing the very best legacy letter possible.*

Planning for Your Pets: *If something were to happen to you, what would happen to them?*

Handwritten Letters to Your Grandchildren: *a keepsake they will treasure their whole life long.*

More titles from Let Family Know®

5.5″ x 8.5″ planners, journals, organizers, keepers

My Important Information ORGANIZER

What I Want You to Have PLANNER

What I Want You to Know JOURNAL

Family, Friends and Others ORGANIZER

My Digital Life USERNAME/PASSWORD ORGANIZER

My Digital Life PRIVATE ACCESS KEEPER

Made in the USA
Monee, IL
04 November 2026

67377634R00118